THE
GLORY
OF
GALATIANS

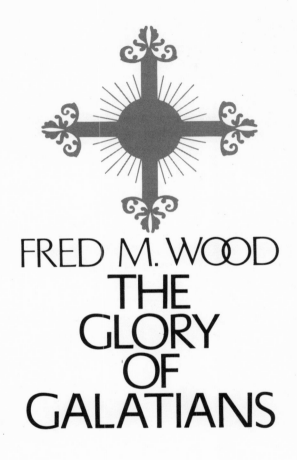

FRED M. WOOD
THE GLORY OF GALATIANS

BROADMAN PRESS / NASHVILLE, TENNESSEE

Dewey Decimal Classification Number: 227.4
Library of Congress Catalog Card Number: 70-178069
Printed in the United States of America

Dedication

Union University, Jackson, Tennessee, has made a unique contribution to the kingdom of God. Thousands of people who were trained at this fine school labor for the Lord in every part of the world. Preachers and laymen alike have secured both academic depth and spiritual ideals in its classrooms.

This book is affectionately dedicated to Union University. All of the author's royalties from the sale of the book will go directly to the expansion and relocation program of Union University with the hope that many others will also support that cause.

Contents

Overview

The book of Galatians has been called "Paul's declaration of religious independence." In this letter he disowns any teaching or custom that threatens or even minimizes the doctrine of "justification by grace apart from the works of man." It is written with such fervor that Winston Pearce calls it a "masterpiece which begins with an earthquake and works up to a climax."

Paul's doctrinal integrity had been assailed! He had been called a false teacher! Not only had his apostolic credentials been questioned, but an innuendo struck at his personal integrity. It is easily understandable why he expressed his feelings in such a way that Charles Jefferson says, "He writes with heat; his language flows like molten lava. The whole letter crashes and echoes like a thunderstorm! He scolds, he pleads, he denounces, he exhorts, he argues, he asserts dogmatically, all in a whirlwind of emotion." The letter has been described as a sword flashing in the hand of an expert fighter. Both Paul and his gospel had been attacked. He must defend himself and the message he proclaimed.

1. Basic Issue of the Book

Although scholars disagree on several matters concerning the letter, there is no doubt about the theme of the book. Paul is writing to state unequivocably the terms on which a sinful person can find acceptance with God.

The first doctrinal controversy that shook the Christian world concerned the relationship of grace and law. The theme of Paul's messages was clear. Man could be justified in only one way—upon the basis of his faith in Christ. Good works issued forth from the life of the believer, but they were the result of his becoming a child of God and not the means. Since this was true, the Christian was free from observing all of the technical laws of the Jewish faith.

1

There was, however, a group of Jewish Christians who did not perceive as plainly as Paul the absolute freedom of the Christian faith from Judaism. To them, Christianity was the fulfilment of the Old Testament, but it was still a part (the best part—but still a part) of the Jewish faith. A Gentile could become a Christian, but first of all he must adopt the Jewish faith and continue in all of the laws of Moses which had guided the Jews for centuries.

Paul immediately recognized Christianity could never be a worldwide religion if it remained circumscribed within the context of Judaism. Salvation by grace meant a believer was a new creation in Christ. He must not be bound by the shackles of ceremonialism and required to obey laws. The believer in Christ must be free to operate within the realm of the spirit and make his choices upon the basis of Christ's personal presence in his life. To Paul, this was the very heart of the Christian faith.

2.   Paul and the Galatian Churches

On his first missionary journey Paul visited the cities of Antioch, Iconium, Lystra, and Derbe. These were in the Roman province of Galatia. Most scholars today take the position that these are the congregations addressed in the letter which Paul wrote to the "churches of Galatia."

There is an alternate theory. On the second missionary journey (Acts 16:6) Paul went "throughout Phrygia and the region of Galatia." He was forbidden by the Holy Spirit to preach in Asia but passed by Mysia and came to Troas. This "region of Galatia" is not to be confused with the Roman province which was formed in 25 B.C. Northern Galatia, as scholars call this area, was settled by a group of Celts or Gauls in the third century B.C. They ravaged much of western Asia Minor and were gradually confined to a district with boundaries set for them. From this came the independent state of Galatia. Thus the term "Galatia" was used in two different senses during the first century. *Geographically,* it designated the country in the northern part of the central plateau of Asia Minor, but *politically* it designated a large province of the Roman Empire established for administrative purposes.

When Paul refers to the "churches of Galatia," is he thinking of churches in the cities of Pessinus, Ancyra, and Tavium, located in the old kingdom of Galatia which may be called North Galatia?

If so, he is writing to churches of which we have no biblical record other than the vague reference in Acts 16:6 and another equally vague one in Acts 18:23 where we are told that Paul began his third missionary journey by going "over all the country of Galatia and Phrygia in order, strengthening all the disciples."

Much has been written concerning this problem. There seems to be a tendency today among scholars to accept the South Galatian theory which means the churches addressed in the letter are those of Antioch, Iconium, Lystra, and Derbe.

3. Date of the Letter

When was the book of Galatians written? In the main, three periods in the life of Paul have been suggested by scholars as the time of composition.

Many scholars believe the letter was written from Corinth on Paul's third missionary journey about the same time as the book of Romans. The similarity of content to Romans is one of the major reasons for this contention. A lesser reason is Paul's excitement over the unfaithfulness of the Galatians to his teachings and the long distance that separated them, making it impossible for him to go there immediately to correct these errors which had arisen. These scholars usually group together 1 and 2 Corinthians, Romans, and Galatians as the four doctrinal letters of Paul and consider all of them as coming from the busy third missionary journey. According to the view of most of these scholars, 1 Corinthians was written from Ephesus during the three-year stay, and 2 Corinthians was written while Paul was in Macedonia after leaving Ephesus. Romans and Galatians were then written during the three months that Paul spent in Corinth.

A second view is that Galatians was written in Ephesus during the three-year period mentioned above. According to Acts 18:23, Paul went through the country of Galatia on his way to Ephesus on the third journey. Most of the scholars who hold this position would probably contend Galatians was written early during the ministry there—before 1 Corinthians, although both were written during the three-year period at Ephesus.

A third view, and one gaining in acceptance today, is that the book was written early—perhaps the first of Paul's letters. It could have been written at the close of the first missionary journey immediately before the Jerusalem Conference (Acts 15), or it could have been written immediately after the Jerusalem Conference. It seems more logical that it would have been written after the conference and shortly before the second missionary journey began. We know Paul visited these churches on his second journey and delivered the decrees of the council at Jerusalem to them. It seems reasonable to believe that Paul wrote on his own apostolic authority immediately after the conference intending to visit them shortly in person. He was fortified by the events that had occurred at the conference and planned to follow up with a visit giving more details. This view is, of course, based on the fact that the churches addressed were those in South Galatia.

4. Structure and Analysis

This is no ordinary letter. It is a controversial pamphlet—intensely polemical. Two things are at stake: first, there is the matter of Paul's apostleship and, second, the nature of the gospel. These two issues give us the basis for the first two main divisions of the letter. The third section consists of an appeal by the apostle for practical Christian living based upon the theological foundation Paul has laid in the other sections.

A simplified approach to an analysis of the book would be to assign two chapters to each of the main subjects discussed. There is, however, an introduction (1:1–10) and a conclusion (6:11–18) that should be set apart from the main outline.

In the introduction Paul immediately comes to the point of his writing. He spends little time in the niceties of salutation. The very first sentence is a harbinger of the argumentative nature of the letter. His apostleship has not come from man but directly from Jesus Christ. Paul is utterly amazed that the Galatians are so fickle they have turned from his message so quickly. Paul offers no compromise nor is he willing to negotiate in any way. Anyone who preaches any other gospel than the one he delivered to them is misleading the people and perverting the true message of Christ.

In the first main division (1:11—2:21) Paul enlarges upon that which he stated at the outset. His gospel has not come from a human source. It has come by special revelation. He reviews his personal experiences with the twelve. He had received a direct message from Christ in his call to service. It was three years later that he went to see Simon Peter and spent some time with him. The only other apostle he saw was James, the brother of the Lord. He preached in Syria and Cilicia but was not even known by the people in the churches of Judea. They only heard of his marvelous conversion and his preaching ministry.

It was fourteen years later that he went to Jerusalem to consult with the leaders there concerning the gospel he was preaching. They made no contribution to his message or the authority by which he preached it. They recognized the validity of his claim to be an apostle to the Gentiles. They extended to him the right hand of fellowship and recognized him as an equal.

Paul's authority was so great that he even dared to condemn Simon Peter, who was considered the chief of the apostles. Paul felt Peter needed the rebuke. Peter had come to Antioch and had joined in the principles advocated by Paul. He had fellowship with the Jews in the eating of food. When the strict Jewish party arrived in Antioch, however, with their insistence that Jewish ceremonial regulations must be held intact, Simon Peter compromised his convictions and withdrew from his fellowship with the Gentile Christians. Paul's boldness in correcting Peter was another evidence that he was on an equal footing with him and not a "second-rate" apostle in any sense of the word.

The second main section (3:1—4:31) deals with the heart of the message. Paul begins with an earnest appeal to the personal experience of the Galatians. They received the Spirit by faith. They should continue to live by faith and not seek justification upon the basis of performing the deeds required in the Mosaic law. He continues his argument by an appeal to history. Abraham was justified by faith. He is a symbol of all believers.

Paul continues his argument by pointing out the nature of the covenant that God made with Abraham. It was not based upon the law because the law came 430 years later. It was based upon faith. The law was given in order to make men realize their guilt and their need of a Savior.

Paul continues the discussion by pointing out the parallel between the person under the law and the child who, while still an heir, must live under proper supervision until the time the testament becomes valid. When the child becomes mature, he may move from strict guardianship to freedom. Likewise, the child of God moves by faith in Christ to spiritual liberty as a mature son.

In the remainder of this large section Paul makes a threefold appeal to the Galatians. He urges them not to consider turning back to the law as spiritual progress. He then adds an appeal to their affection. They had loved him and respected him in his previous encounters with them. He is unable to understand why they have rebelled against him as a person and ceased to follow his spiritual leadership. His final appeal is to their rationality. Since they think so much of the law, they should examine the basic teaching of the law concerning enslavement and liberty. The two sons of Abraham illustrate his message. Which son became their heir? Was it the child of the slave or the child of the free woman? Likewise, Christians are made for liberty not for enslavement.

When we come to the third main division (5:1—6:10), the letter changes its emphasis. Paul has been theological. He moves now into the ethical and moral realm. Some scholars place 5:1–12 in the preceding section since it still is argumentative in nature, contending for freedom from the shackles of legalism. In this section he warns of the perils in accepting circumcision. He argues that it will obligate them to the entire Mosaic system. Paul contended that the way of faith and the way of law are mutually exclusive. It must be "either-or." It cannot be "both-and." Paul assures the Galatians their confidence in the law did not come from him. Someone has sown the seed of false teaching among them. He urges the Galatians to root out this false teaching before it pollutes and destroys their entire religious faith.

Beginning with 5:13 the ethical content of the book comes into full focus. Paul never considered theology an end in itself. Its purpose was to provide a base for living out one's faith in the world. He scaled the heights of theological thinking, but he always ended his letters with an appeal to righteous living motivated by a loving spirit. The Galatians are free, but their liberty is not to be treated as license for selfish indulgence. A great battle is going on in the life of the believer; the flesh and the spirit are constantly at warfare. Paul lists the works of the flesh and the works of the spirit. He urges that the one living in the spirit must show in his life the lovely things which have come to fruition because Christ dwells in the heart. He maintains the believer's life is energized by the Holy Spirit.

The secret of all Paul is urging is to be found in "liberty perfected by love." He closes this main section with two specific illustrations. First, the believer will help others when they are at fault, remembering always the possibility of his own stumbling. Second, the believer, because of his love, will share his good things with those who guide him in his Christian life. At this point, Paul is intensely practical. He believes the spiritual worker is worthy of being supported financially by the congregation. This section concludes with Paul reminding the Galatians of the grim truth that the law of sowing and reaping works with precision and accuracy. The mill of God grinds slowly but it grinds exceedingly thorough. The Christian, therefore, must continue without weariness. He must do good to everyone but be especially related to those who are his brothers in Christ.

The conclusion (6:11–18) was probably written by Paul's own hand. Some scholars think the whole letter may have come from the apostle's personal penmanship. He concludes by affirming afresh his condemnation of the Judaizers and insists, in the last heartbeat of his letter, that his entire allegiance is to the cross of Christ and the Christ of the cross. Those who follow this discipline are truly the Israel of God. Paul closes with an affirmation of independence based on his personal dedication to Christ.

5. Value for Today

It is immediately obvious that the *exact and specific* problem dealt with in the book of Galatians is not an issue in contemporary Christianity. There is no Judaizing party haunting the ministry of Christian evangelists insisting that Gentiles today must become Jews before they can become Christians.

On the other hand, the *basic* issue of this letter is perhaps the most controversial in Christendom today. Actually, there are only two schools of thought as to how man can be justified in the sight of God. On the one hand, there are those who teach that salvation from the penalty of sin comes upon the basis of good deeds. It is how a man lives that gains for him a right standing before God. On the other hand, there is that great school of Christianity which insists that man's good works do not justify, nor do they help to keep justified, the sinner in the sight of God. Guilty man is made

righteous in the sight of God only by accepting the righteousness
of God in Jesus Christ. These two schools of thought form the basis
for the division of theological camps in current Christian thinking.

Paul's Galatian letter is superlatively relevant for the theological
fragmentation present in modern Christendom. It insists that we
neither become a Christian nor remain a Christian by the obeying
of certain laws or the performance of certain church rituals. Religious conditions are different from the day in which Judaism
served as a basis for morality in the religious world. The basic
principle, however, is the same. Religious conscience has placed
approval on some things and disapproval on other things. The
tendency of many is to associate being a Christian with the doing
or not doing of these things. The teaching of Galatians is that man
cannot depend upon a legal code to decide matters of morality
for him. He must be anchored to Christ by faith and then must
make intelligent choices based upon his relationship with God in
Christ. This is the very essence of Christianity.

As long as there is a struggle between the works of the flesh and
the works of the spirit, the book of Galatians will serve as a spiritual
guide for sincere followers of Christ. Ethics and morals are rooted
in a proper theological understanding of the basic truths of God's
revelation in Jesus Christ. On the other hand, as the final section
shows, one properly related to God through faith in Christ, will
not fail to "by love serve one another" and be "led of the Spirit"
into personal maturity. It is no wonder that G. G. Findlay begins
his marvelous work on Galatians in *The Expositor's Bible* with the
statement that "antiquity has nothing to show more notable in its
kind, or more precious, than this letter of Paul to the Churches
of Galatia."

Introduction

1:1–10

After a very brief salutation, Paul plunges into that which will be the thrust of his letter. The source of salvation is in Christ. He is completely adequate for every need of the human heart. Although his deepest convictions had been challenged, Paul would not give one inch of ground in his contention that the gospel of Christ was as he had preached it, and any variance from his message was heresy serious enough to demand that one be excluded from the Christian fellowship.

1. Salutation (1:1–3)

1:1—Paul: This was his Gentile name. He is called Saul in the book of Acts until 13:9 when the transition was made by Luke. From then on he is "Paul" and also he takes precedence over Barnabas in most cases when they are listed together. It was customary for one in bilingual situations to adopt a name in keeping with the people among whom he was working or serving. In the earlier part of his life Paul was a Jew among Jews. Thus he was "Saul." William Ramsay quotes Lewin as saying, "The dropping of the Jewish, and the adoption of a Roman name, was in harmony with the great truth he was promulgating—that henceforth the partition between Jew and Gentile was broken down." Saul became Paul when he stood by himself in the Gentile world and became the principal factor.

Apostle: The word literally means "sent from." Some would translate it "envoy." In the broad and general sense the word means anyone who is sent forth with an accredited message or on a special mission. In the Christian sense *anyone* sent forth with the message of Christ would be an apostle. In the more restricted sense, however, the word seems to have come to be used for the original twelve. It was Paul's contention he was as much of an

9

apostle as any of the twelve. Many scholars believe Simon Peter rushed matters in insisting on electing a successor for Judas. They insist Saul of Tarsus was the one God chose to complete the twelve. Paul never makes such a statement but probably would have agreed to it—at least in his early ministry when he was defending his apostleship so vehemently.

Not of men, neither by man: The first phrase denies that his calling was of human origin. He had been laid hold of by God and given a direct commission from God. It was on the Damascus Road that he received this initial call. He refers to it in his speech before Agrippa (Acts 26:16–18). The second phrase speaks of instrumentality. He excludes all men from any agency in his appointment to his apostolic office. No body of men sent him out. He did not receive his commission or authority through the medium of human agency. Today a preacher receives his call from God, but he is usually ordained by a human agency. Matthias was certainly a God-called man, but he was voted by the eleven to be a member of their group. Timothy was likewise God-called but he was appointed to his office. The presbytery laid their hands on him (1 Tim. 4:14). Paul received no such recognition from men. It is true he, along with Barnabas, had been set apart by the brethren at Antioch (Acts 13:1–3), but this was for a special mission in Asia Minor. It was not an appointment to his apostleship. Paul's call was from God and likewise his commission was from God.

By Jesus Christ, and God the Father: Paul uses here only one preposition for God and Jesus Christ. If he had wished to parallel this phrase with the preceding clause, he would have added another preposition. He, however, uses the preposition here that he used for the second phrase above which signified instrumentality or channel more than source. Lukyn Williams in *Galatians* of the "Cambridge Greek Testament" suggests this is probably because of his "vivid sense of the unity of the two Persons." Lightfoot comments, "The channel of his authority coincides with its source." It may be that Jesus is mentioned here first because he appeared to Paul.

Who raised him from the dead: Literally, "out of the region of the dead ones." Paul wishes for the readers to grasp the greatness of Christ's work. He feels the Judaizers have failed to emphasize the tremendous achievement of Christ in his resurrection, and this has blurred the true power of the risen and exalted Lord. It is not the birth or even the death of Christ, important as these are, that furnishes the dynamic of the Christian message and attests to the sufficiency of Christ for salvation. It is his *resurrection* by which we are justified. Paul said elsewhere concerning Jesus that he "was delivered for our offenses, and was raised again for our justification" (Rom. 4:25).

1:2—All the brethren which are with me: Paul means all the believers in the place from which he was writing his letter. In Galatians he seems to mean his special friends and workers who were with him at that particular time. Why did he not name them? It may be that he felt so strongly about the matter concerning which he was writing that he purposely avoided naming any of his associates who might, if challenged, yield somewhat on the position. Paul was a rugged individualist and, especially in this situation, wanted to state his position firmly with no chance of anyone watering it down unless they faced Paul personally and refuted his arguments. It may be, of course, on the other hand, that Paul included the phrase "all the brethren" because he wanted to make it a team decision and omitted the names because there was such a large number of people with him at the time. Since we cannot be certain as to the place from which the letter was written, we also cannot be sure as to who the "brethren" are to whom Paul refers.

The churches of Galatia: This phrase has puzzled scholars. Certainly Paul is referring to local churches. The Greek word for church means literally "called out," and although the word was used to refer to non-Christian assemblies (even in the New Testament, see Acts 19:41), Christianity has given it a distinctive meaning. The perplexity of scholars is not with reference to the meaning of the word but to the matter of which churches Paul is addressing. If he is writing to the churches of Northern Galatia (see Overview), he is probably referring here to the churches at Pessimus, Ancyra, and Tavium. If we accept the South Galatian theory, he is addressing the churches of Antioch, Iconium, Derbe, and Lystra. This could be considered a circular letter, since it was for all of the churches. We do not know whether several copies were made or whether Paul intended for the one copy to be circulated among the churches. The probability is there was only one copy made since Paul refers to writing with his own hand in Galatians 6:11. We do not know whether he was referring to the entire letter being written by his own hand or whether he was referring to a few words at the end which he wrote in large letters (see commentary on 6:11). Since the churches of Galatia were, no doubt, close to each other and had the same general characteristics, we can easily see that they had probably fallen into the same errors and, therefore, the same letter would be sufficient for all of them. This is why he writes only one letter to them whether he made extra copies of it or not.

1:3—Grace: Theologically, the word means free and unmerited love or undeserved generosity. There is also within it the idea of "sheer beauty." Barclay says it always has within it the idea of beauty and charm. He says that when Paul prays for grace it is as though he said, "May the beauty of the wonder of the undeserved love of God be on you, so that it will make your life lovely too."

Peace: Even today the customary word of greeting for the Jew to his friend is "Shalom." In modern Israel the Jews use it and the Arabs have a word which is very similar to it that they use in greeting. The word means more than the absence of unpleasant things. When the Jew says "Shalom," he means "May the very finest things in life come to you. May your mind be clear, your will firm, and may your heart be filled with gladness and joy." Some scholars believe Paul used this word because his mind was "dominated by the thought of the admission of the Gentiles to the privileges which had been peculiar to Israel." The apostle was certainly conscious that he was using a Jewish formula for his Gentile friends to express God's encircling protection for those who were in Christ.

Lord Jesus Christ: The use of this phrase would lay a foundation for laying stress on Christ's work of salvation. The Eastern world was familiar with the expression. To them it was a divine predicate and there was no possibility the implication would be unintelligible to his readers.

2.   In Praise of Jesus Christ (1:4–5)

1:4—Who gave himself for our sins: Paul immediately introduces Christ's atoning work. It is, of course, the basis for the doctrine of justification by faith which was Paul's fundamental contention in this letter. When one understands the significance of Christ's death as the central act in redemption, he sees how unnecessary, as well as how inadequate, human activity is either to bring or to sustain a new standing before God. Paul may be echoing the saying of Jesus in Matthew 20:28 and Mark 10:45 where we are told Christ "gave himself a ransom for many." The Greek preposition translated "for" has the idea of "on behalf of" and is also used in his first letter to Timothy (2:6) and Titus (2:14).

Deliver us from this present evil world: To Paul, the present age was one in which sin and death ruled. It was under the sway of principalities and powers. He refers in Romans 8:2 to "the law of sin and death." In the great redemptive act of Christ we are rescued from this sphere of living and transplanted over into a new way of life. Paul refers to it in Romans 8:2 as "the law of the spirit of life in Christ Jesus." The verb signifies "rescue" and does not mean "to take away by death" or "to remove to another world" but rather to remove sinners from a living dominated by the sinful world and place them in an environment controlled and motivated by God in Jesus Christ.

According to the will of God: This was rooted in the eternal purpose of God. It was not devised nor was it executed by human wisdom. Man is not capable of such a profound work. Only an infinite mind could conceive such a great salvation and only an infinite power, which nothing could frustrate or hinder, could implement it.

1:5—To whom be glory forever: This is not so much an ascription as it is a glad affirmation. We might compare it with the ending of the "Lord's Prayer." In the original text the reading is *"the* glory" and refers to that which is especially God's and belongs alone to him. The salutation is thus enriched by Paul's ejaculation of praise. Alan Cole points out that the Greek word used here is not the word signifying the empty praise that man can give. It is rather the word that translates a Hebrew word referring to the unutterable effulgence of the divine glory that to a Jew denoted the very presence of God.

3. Circumstances Which Made the Letter Necessary
(1:6–10)

1:6—I marvel: The apostle has managed to keep back his strong feeling long enough to greet the Galatians with a generous and tactful salutation. But his intense and painful anxiety must be

expressed. The word of greeting was adequate but he had omitted
some of his customary words of thanksgiving for such things as
fellowship, achievements of the church, and prospects for further
growth. Paul plunged into the problem concerning which he was
writing with an abrupt and passionate outburst. He raises the issue
at once because his heart is full. The painful and even dangerous
alienation between Paul and the people of Galatia must be met
head on and immediately. He does, however, restrain himself
enough to use what Martin Luther calls "as mild a word as possible." Barnes says, "He does not employ the language of severe
reproof, but he expresses his astonishment that the thing should
have occurred. He was deeply affected and amazed, that such a
thing could have happened."

So soon removed: Most scholars take the position that the translation should be "so quickly" and refers not to the brevity of time
but to the "rapidity with which they are yielding to the temptation." It is impossible to decide the date of the epistle upon the
basis of the time element. The "soon" or "quickly" could easily
refer to the rapidity with which the Galatians had yielded after
the Judaizers came along and began their work. The verb
"removed" is in the present tense which, in Greek, indicates a
process that is still taking place. Paul is hoping he is not too late
to stop the "mind changing" of the Galatians.

Him that called you: The one calling them was not Paul. It was
God. Paul was the messenger who had brought the good news.
The people had done more than leave a doctrinal belief. They had
deserted the God who had revealed himself in Jesus Christ. The
verb is not present (which would indicate action in progress) but
an aorist participle which indicates "point action." There is an
element of finality here. God has called them "once and for all."

1:7—Another gospel . . . Which is not another: Two separate
Greek words are translated with the same word in English. This
change of words on the part of Paul has caused scholars to comment at length concerning Paul's sharp contrast of meaning. The
old traditional distinction was that the first *(heteros)* means a difference in kind while the second *(allos)* means a difference in
number. On this basis Paul would be saying that they have turned
to a different kind of gospel but that it is not in reality a true gospel.
Paul called it "a gospel" because it pretended to be, but it was

actually a proclamation which, if accepted, destroyed the grace of God in Christ because it placed upon them the burdensome ceremonies of which the true gospel of Christ graciously relieved them. It is true that these two words are used in 2 Corinthians 11:4 and 1 Corinthians 12:9 ff. for variation without any seeming significance. Yet, in this context Paul does seem to be drawing a distinction even in the use of words. The gospel (so called) to which the Galatians were turning was not really a gospel in a qualitative sense. It does not exist as a true gospel. Paul rejects the whole idea of another gospel. This is certainly what Paul is saying and there is strong reason to believe there is a profound significance in his choice of the two words for "another." There is no other gospel to be placed alongside his true gospel. The people do not have an alternate choice. The message of the Judaizers is only a spurious semblance and an unworthy substitute.

Some that trouble you: There seems to be a deliberate vagueness concerning the identification of the agitators. They certainly were not Galatian Christians. Paul uses the plural here while elsewhere in the letter he uses the singular. There is probably no particular significance to this except that the Judaizers may have had one strong leader to whom he referred in particular. The word translated "trouble" has been rendered *harass, stir up, agitate physically, disturb* (mentally and spiritually), and *excite* (with fear). This verb is used in Acts 17:8 where it is said that the Jews in Thessalonica "troubled [disturbed] the people and the rulers of the city."

Would pervert the gospel: A. T. Robertson says, "The very existence of the gospel of Christ was at stake." The opponents were in the very act of destroying everything for which Paul had worked. The word means literally "to turn about" (change completely). The same word is used in Acts 2:20, "The sun shall be turned into darkness" and in James 4:9 "let your laughter be turned to mourning." Of course, the Judaizers could not pervert the *gospel*. They could only pervert those who were professing faith in the gospel. They could dilute the message and change it and thus mislead the people. Paul's hearers, however, would understand his meaning even as we do. We often use the expression "break a law" when we realize, with a little contemplation, that we cannot "break a law" but rather we "break ourselves on the

law." The law stands. So, the gospel stands as the gospel. People
are merely misled when the message is proclaimed falsely.

1:8—An angel from heaven: The Greek word for angel means
literally messenger. This was probably Paul's meaning. He could
have been referring, however, to the common belief of the Jews
that the law had been given to the people through angelic media-
tors. Since the Judaizers were stressing the keeping of the law, the
reference would be relevant. Again, Paul could have been referring to the possibility that Satan himself was appearing to the
Galatian Christians as an angel of light and seeking to mislead
them. Paul, of course, feels very strongly about the statement he
is about to make. He includes himself in the declaration. If he were
to reverse his position, the people are warned that they should
ostracize him.

Let him be accursed: The Greek word *anathema* (for "accursed") translates the Hebrew *herem*. Snaith believes the original
meaning of the root was probably "refuse, forbid," without any
particular religious significance in the developed sense of the
word "religious." The word developed along what we would call
secular lines but then came to refer to that which had been set
apart to a god other than Jehovah. It could be "devoted" to Jehovah by being utterly, completely, and ruthlessly destroyed. When
someone was ordered by Jehovah "to devote to destruction" something, he must fulfil this dedication. He was "under the curse" (see
Josh. 7:1). That which was "holy" to Jehovah was *cherem* to another god and that which was "holy" to another god was *cherem*
to Jehovah. The Greek word *anathema* (used here in Galatians)
has grown out of this word *herem* of the Old Testament. A thing
set apart was banned. It was cut off from anything else. From this
comes the idea of a thing cut off from divine mercy and exposed
to the full sweep of judgment. It is in this last sense that Paul is
using the word "anathema." The people of Paul's day would turn
in horror from either an object or a man who was "under the
curse" or "under the wrath of God." This type of curse was un-
believably horrible for another reason. The thing or person accursed was unconditionally doomed to destruction because in Jewish thinking when once the curse was uttered it could not be
recalled even by the one who spoke it.

1:9—As we said before, so say I now again: There have been two interpretations of this phrase. One is that Paul is repeating for emphasis the thing he has just written. He repeated it because of its importance. He wants to deepen the impression he had made and wants to be certain he is not misunderstood. Perhaps Paul anticipated that some might try to soften his words and lighten the weight of the awful sentence he had written. The repetition of the word is not like a man in a passion who flings out his words as missiles, wishing only to wound and confound the opposition. He repeats the sentence coolly and calmly. The words reflect well weighted thought and judicial solemnity. He is acting under the sense of his apostolic responsibility. These opponents of his gospel were opponents of Christ. Paul had no alternative. He must hurl his anathema at anyone who opposes the gospel of Christ even if that person should be the prince of the archangels. The other view is that Paul is referring to the preaching of himself and his companions on a previous visit to Galatia. Those who hold this view point out that he uses the plural in speaking of the previous exhortation. They contend this implies the earlier warnings were given jointly by Paul and his companions. It is of no theological import as to which of these views is correct. It would not be fair to say that scholars in general lean to either one of these interpretations. This writer prefers the first.

1:10—Do I now persuade men: Moffatt translates "Now is that 'appealing to the interest of men' or of God?" According to him, this tenth verse should be considered very closely with the preceding verses rather than with the next section. Paul realizes he has used strong language. He is pointing out that his uncompromising boldness should convince anyone that he is not a "time server" saying one thing with one group of people and another thing with another group. He has positioned himself (even in writing). The whole world may now know his position. If he were a man pleaser, he would try to straddle the fence but he is throwing himself completely on the side of "salvation by grace and grace alone." This, he is convinced, is the message of Christ for a lost world. He denied that he was trying to ingratiate himself with men or curry their favor by diluting the message.

Servant of Christ: There are several Greek words in the New Testament which are translated "servant" but the one used here is the most meaningful of all. It is the Greek word *doulos* which

Paul always uses to express his relationship to Christ as servant. This word means a "bond slave." Paul considered himself a slave that had been bought and paid for by Jesus Christ. He belonged to Christ. He was not working for wages as a household servant works, but he was laboring for Christ because he was completely owned by the Savior. Jesus was not only his Savior from sin but also the Lord of his life.

I. Paul's Defense of His Apostleship
1:11 to 2:21

In several passages of this larger section Paul defends his right to consider himself on equal authority with the apostles. The events which immediately followed Paul's conversion proved no man was his teacher concerning the gospel. He was originally a persecutor of the Christians. He had been one who excelled in obeying all the technical requirements of legal religion. When God arrested him in his fanatical activity and revealed Jesus Christ to him, he did not consult with any human being. Neither did he go to Jerusalem to have a conference with those who had been apostles longer than he. He went rather to Arabia and then returned to Damascus. It was three years before he went up to Jerusalem to see Peter. Later he visited Syria and Cilicia but was personally unknown to the membership of the churches of Judea.

Fourteen years later Paul went again to Jerusalem. This time he took Barnabas and Titus with him. He gave a full explanation to the people there of the gospel as he preached it among the Gentiles. He did not consider them his superiors. He went as an equal and discussed the gospel with them as one who had the right to share his views and be accepted in his own person. Later, Paul went so far as to criticize Peter for an action in Antioch. He insisted to Peter that the Jews had no right to force upon the Gentiles many things that they themselves did not observe. This section closes with a strong defense of justification by faith apart from the works of the law and a testimony of the presence of the indwelling Christ in the life of Paul.

1. His Gospel Was Directly from Christ (1:11–12)

1:11—I certify you, brethren: This expression introduces a declaration which is more solemn than usual. Paul must make it clear to them. There can be no misunderstanding. Paul, at different times, uses various expressions with which he introduces such solemn statements. This one is direct and forceful.

Brethren: This word is used no less than nine times in this letter. It seems to indicate a personal and individual acquaintance. Paul does not consider them as having unqualifiedly rejected the gospel of God's grace. They are, perhaps, on the brink of doing this since they are certainly looking in the wrong direction and giving ear to those who are misleading them. If they continue in this dangerous error, the result can be tragic. Yet the whole tone of this letter is that he is seeking to bring them back to full confidence in Jesus as their completely sufficient Savior. Thus he addresses them as brethren. Although the letter is serious and argumentative, the tone is friendly. Paul still considers them as his followers and is anxious to reestablish the relationship between them and him as one of full confidence and mutual understanding.

Gospel . . . not after man: This phrase is stronger than "after the tradition of men" (Col. 2:8) or "the doctrine of men" (Col. 2:22). It is far above anything man could conceive. It is out of the realm of the human. No human instructor had made it known to Paul. It had not been debased or adulterated by any human contribution. Paul's message was directly from Jesus Christ.

Which was preached of me: Literally, Paul said "the gospel which was gospelized by me." The noun and verb are both built on the same root which means "good news."

1:12—The revelation of Jesus Christ: The Greek word means literally, an uncovering, unveiling, or disclosing. There is a dispute among scholars as to whether the phrase "of Jesus Christ" should be a subjective genitive or an objective genitive. Was Jesus Christ the one who made the revelation to Paul or, rather than preceding from Jesus, was this a disclosure of religious truth about Jesus which was before unknown by Paul. In a sense, both are true and perhaps as Alan Cole suggests it is better to "leave the ambiguity in the English as it is in the Greek." There seems a little preference on the part of most scholars to believe the emphasis is on the content rather than the source of revelation but one should not necessarily eliminate the other.

2.   Superiority in the Jewish Faith (1:13–14)

1:13—My conversation: Originally, the verb root from which this noun comes meant "return" or "turning back." It came to mean, however, "the going up and down among men in the various intercourses of life" from which we get the idea of "mode of life." It is more than mere behavior since this suggests only external action. It has to do with one's entire approach to and philosophy of life.

In the Jews' religion: This refers to his belief in and practice of what we today call Judaism. This included not only the religion of Moses but all of the interpretations and oral traditions of the Jews down to his day. Although it was a bit later before Judaism and Christianity began to be used in diametrical opposition to each other, it is evident here that Paul already understands that they are separate religions. The author of the Fourth Gospel uses the expression "the Jews" almost synonymous with those opposed to Christianity (John 10:31). Alan Cole says, "The rejection of their Promised Messiah had turned Judaism from the main course of God's plan and purpose to a stagnant back water."

I persecuted the church of God and wasted it: Although Paul calls himself "the chief of sinners" (1 Tim. 1:15), he was not a man of moral turpitude and degradation. He was rather a hardheaded, overbearing, intolerant egoist in his religious life. His determined and pitiless oppression was unequalled in the history of Judaism. He was the forerunner of the fanatical Jews who later sought his life when he became a Christian. Paul suffered remorse all of his Christian life because of his persecution of the Christians before his own conversion. This Greek word for persecuted is also used by Luke (Acts 9:4) in recording the words of Jesus "Saul, Saul, why persecutest thou me?" In all probability, Paul could not use this word without being reminded most vividly of the Damascus Road experience. The word translated "wasted" is the one used for utterly sacking a city. Barclay uses the expression "try to make a scorched earth of the Church."

Ye have heard: It may be that Paul had told the Galatians with his own mouth of his pre-Christian days as he related his experience of conversion to them. Twice in the book of Acts (Acts 22 and 26) is found the recital of his conversion experience. On the other hand, the Galatians may have received the news from other Christians as the story of Paul's conversion spread from church to church. For such an outstanding opponent of the Christian faith to be converted in such a miraculous way must have made a tremendous impression upon all of the country. There also is the

possibility that the Judaizers themselves may have told the Galatians in a scornful way, in order to reinforce their message, that
Paul was but a novice and not actually mature enough in the faith
to speak with any authority.

1:14—Profited in the Jews' religion: Moffatt suggests "out-
stripped many of my Jewish contemporaries" as a more literal
translation. This brilliant young man had an intensely competitive
spirit. He was a foreign Jew, having come from Tarsus, and no
doubt was highly compulsive as he sought to prove himself equal
or superior to the best of the Palestinians. The Greek word translated "profited" is from an old verb which meant "to cut forward"
(as in a forest) or "to blaze a way" and from this we get the idea
of to "move ahead." Paul was undoubtedly one of Gamaliel's star
pupils. It is doubtful, however, if Gamaliel approved of Paul's zeal
in persecuting the church (Acts 5:38). This might indicate that
Paul considered that he was even a more devout Jew than
Gamaliel. Tennyson has a line in one of his poems which says "The
pupil outran the teacher." This could well apply to the relationship between Paul and Gamaliel.

Above many my equals: There may be a bit of modesty here.
He probably could have said "all my equals." The true sense of
the original probably means those equal in years. There seems no
doubt he would have been superior to any of his own age. Surely
no one had the scholarly depth for understanding the law nor the
passionate intensity to see it enforced!

3.   Paul's Conversion and What Followed (1:15–17)

**1:15—It pleased God who separated me from my mother's
womb:** Although Paul brought a rich background of Judaism to
Christ, he never failed to realize that he was, like Isaac, a man of
promise. Paul never attempts to explain his belief in God's elective
grace. He merely states it as a fact. Paul would have been the last
person in the world to deny the free will of man. Yet he, at the
same time, and without any consciousness of inconsistency, accepted the complete sovereignty of God in all things.

Paul is not suggesting that he had actually been called to his
work while an infant but rather that in the supernatural wisdom
of God he had a purpose for Paul from his very birth. Many of
God's great servants have felt they were chosen by God from the

beginning. Albert Barnes says, "We should never despair of a young man who has wandered far from God. If he has risen high in attainment; if his whole aim is ambition; or if he has become an infidel, still we are not to despair of him. It is *possible* still that God 'separated' that talent to his service from the very birth and that he means yet to call it all to his service. How easy it was to convert Saul of Tarsus when the proper period arrived." Notice the unique parallel of Paul with Jeremiah. God said to the Old Testament prophet, "Before I formed thee in the belly, I knew thee; and before thou camest forth out of the womb I sanctified thee, and I ordained thee a prophet unto the nations" (Jer. 1:5).

His grace: The classic definition of grace is "the free and unmerited love and mercy of God." To Paul, it was more. It was the key both to the nature of God and the personality of man. It was the secret of his new life. Through it he was brought an entirely new conception of God and, therefore, of himself. Forgiveness has been called "the profoundest moral fact of all time." If this is true, the grace of God is the highest expression of this forgiveness and is the strongest moral power available for the transformation of man. Grossly wicked lives have been changed by grace and young sensitive souls have been spared a life of shame and disgrace because of its preventive power. Young, eager spirits feeling an inadequacy to face life have been made strong by its enabling force. Human personality is not minimized by this concept of grace but is rather enriched.

Paul's entire personality was integrated and fulfilled because of Christ's grace. He moved from the realm of conceiving of God as a taskmaster who paid strictly for performed services to a friend who indwelt and motivated. He moved from mere abstract obedience to a fellowship of personal companionship and living union with God through Jesus Christ his highest revelation. His religious life became not a book of rules but rather personal attachment to one who redeemed him from sin and made him a new creation.

1:16—To reveal his Son in me: Because of the words that follow this phrase, some wish to translate it "through me" but this is not what the Greek preposition means. *The New English Bible* translates "to me and through me" but this is not a literal translation. It is reading more into the text than is there and is interpreting Paul to say something that he would probably have agreed with

but did not actually say. It is certainly true that the revelation of
Christ to Paul was in order that it could become a revelation of
Christ in Paul to others because the Spirit of God produces fruits
in unlikely soil. The context of the passage, however, as well as
the text make it clear that Paul is telling of a revelation God made
to him—in his own soul. Paul is emphasizing the reality of the
inward experience rather than stressing the external phenomena
accompanying it. It was through this revelation that Paul became
acquainted with Jesus in order that he might understand his true
nature.

That I might preach him among the heathen: The purpose of
this miraculous manifestation is now set forth. The word "heathen" might better be translated "foreigners." Literally, it means
"the peoples," that is, the non-Jewish peoples. Since the verb is
in the present or linear action, it implies an action that is still
continuing. The commission which was given to him was still in
effect. His spiritually renovated nature showed the evidence and
authority of his divine commission. The great spiritual change that
had been wrought in him had inspired him to be a witness to the
Gentile world. The dazzling appearance of Christ remained with
him and the trumpet call of his voice which Paul heard with his
bodily ears continued to ring in his heart. It had pleased God to
call him to be an apostle and Paul had no alternatives or options.
He must obey.

I conferred not with flesh and blood: It is always good to seek
the counsel of wise men. Under ordinary conditions Paul might
have diligently sought and thoughtfully pondered what Peter,
James, and the others advised. But in Paul's unique case he refused
to confer with others lest it be interpreted that he was depending
on human standards for his authority. Paul felt the infinite realities
of the spiritual world, the sanctions of eternity, and the powers
of life to come had been revealed to him by Christ in a way that
gave him equal standing with the other apostles. He thus had
instruments to work with which made all other means and methods seem feeble.

**1:17—Neither went I up to Jerusalem . . . but I went into
Arabia:** The account of Paul's conversion and immediate activity
is condensed quite precisely in the ninth chapter of Acts. After
Paul was baptized, Luke says, "Then was Saul certain days with

the disciples which were at Damascus." The next verse says that immediately he preached in the synagogues. This certainly verifies Paul's statement here that he did not go up to Jerusalem immediately. When was his first trip to Jerusalem? Acts 9:23 ff. tells how the Jews tried to kill Saul but the disciples let him down by the wall in a basket and he came to Jerusalem. He endeavored to join himself to the disciples there, but they were afraid of him until Barnabas recommended him. He was then, for a period of time, with them "coming in and going out at Jerusalem." He spoke so boldly that there was an attempt to take his life there. His Christian friends "brought him down to Caesarea, and sent him forth to Tarsus." We have no further record of Paul until Acts 11:25 when Barnabas left Antioch and went to Tarsus to get Saul to come and help him with the work at Antioch. This was a considerable period of time, and we may be sure that Paul was active in studying the Old Testament in the light of his new experience with Jesus.

One cannot be dogmatic about Paul's activities. The old school of thought pictured Paul going into Arabia and spending three years at Mount Sinai restudying his Old Testament in the light of his new conversion experience. If this be accepted as legitimate interpretation, Paul could have gone to Arabia during the "certain days" of Acts 9:19 but verse 20 seems to indicate that he began preaching rather quickly after his conversion. The "many days" of Acts 9:23 could be the three years in Arabia. Again, after he was sent to Tarsus, as recorded in Acts 9:30, he could have made a three-year trip for his "post-graduate studies" at Sinai.

Most modern scholars, however, do not accept the school of thought which calls for a three-year extended session in Arabia around Sinai. They point out that the area around Damascus was under the rule of Aretas at this time and suggest Paul wandered through various parts of the large kingdom of the Nabateans. During these days it extended from Damascus all the way to the Sinaitic Peninsula. Most modern scholars would probably insist that he did not go very far from Damascus. Then, too, they ask whether the "after three years" of verse 18 mean that he spent three years in Arabia. He could have spent a short time in Arabia and spent the rest of the time in Damascus or at least quite close by the city.

4. His Later Visit to Jerusalem (1:18-19)

1:18—I went up . . . to see Peter: This visit is unrecorded in Acts. If we follow the old interpretation, Paul came to Jerusalem after spending three years meditating in Sinai. He would want to have fellowship with this man who knew Jesus so well, and there would be nothing wrong with this from the standpoint of Saul's authority being questioned. It would be only natural that he might share with Peter some of his convictions about the Old Testament in light of his new discovery that Jesus of Nazareth was the fulfilment of the messianic prophecies. If, on the other hand, we do not accept the fact that Paul spent three years in Arabia (either in Sinai or in the larger Nabatean kingdom), we would probably consider this visit as occurring after Paul was sent back to Tarsus (Acts 9:30) by the brethren at Jerusalem. It is certainly not the "Jerusalem Conference" as recorded in Acts 15. Neither is there evidence that it is the trip of Acts 11:29-30. Of course, we cannot say absolutely that this visit is not the one of Acts 9:23, but the account in Acts does not read as though it were a visit to consult with Peter since Paul was not even accepted by the brethren until Barnabas interceded for him. Paul seemingly does not even refer to this as a visit to Jerusalem. He ignores it in recounting the chronology of his life. This visit to see Peter seems to have been a formal one where he visited with Peter in a quiet and meditative way. The account in Acts 9:26-30 seems to have been one filled with much preaching activity.

Although this writer may be putting himself out on a limb, he wishes to state that he has not yet been convinced that Paul did not make a three-year trip to Sinai and visit Peter on his return from there. It may not be true that he did, but modern scholars have not proved that to this writer's satisfaction.

1:19—James the Lord's brother: In this verse and the one preceding it we gain the impression that Peter was the one to whom Paul was attracted rather than James. Peter seems to have been the principal figure among the apostles. He was an outspoken person—a natural leader. James, on the other hand, did not become a follower of Christ until after the resurrection. He was more conservative and seems to have been the leader of the group that was more closely oriented to the old Hebrew faith. It is perhaps not fair to say that he was in sympathy with the Judaizers, but he probably would be more inclined to give a sympathetic ear to them. It is quite significant that James was able to emerge as the leader of the Jerusalem church and become one of the acknowledged authorities. The fact that he was the brother (actually half-brother) of the Lord must have helped him to attain this position.

Was James actually "an apostle" in the same sense as the others? He certainly was not one of the original twelve. He did not meet the requirements Peter established in Acts 1:21–22. It may be that because of his unique relationship to Jesus he was granted the courtesy of being called an apostle. On the other hand, grammarians have suggested that the word translated "except" may be translated "only." If this be accepted, Paul would not be calling James an apostle but rather saying that the only one of the apostles he saw was Peter but incidentally he did see James.

5. Paul's Further Activity and Reputation (1:20–24)

1:20—Before God, I lie not: Paul considered these things he had been discussing as matters of life and death in the proving of his independence. He had stated the facts bluntly and perhaps realized that to some they might seem unlikely. He felt the necessity, therefore, for a solemn appeal to God in order to remove any suspicion of falsehood. We should remember that this oath does not refer merely to the fact that he was with Peter and James only fifteen days, but it refers to all of the facts he had stated in this chapter thus far. The force of the oath also extends to the following statement also. It is difficult for us to realize what an important issue this was to Paul. To him, the whole truth of his apostleship depended on whether or not he had had prolonged interviews with the leaders of the Jerusalem church before he formulated the message he preached. Since there were not witnesses to whom he could appeal, he appealed directly to God. The amazing truth is that, although Paul had consulted no one, his message harmonized completely with that taught by the other apostles. This was the crux of the matter. God had made a supernatural revelation to Paul and Paul was preaching this gospel which he received directly from God. It was important—to Paul, it was absolutely imperative—that the people accept his word at face value.

1:21—Afterwards . . . Syria and Cilicia: It is difficult to fit this into the chronology of Acts because of the meager records we have. In Acts 9:30 Paul was taken from Jerusalem and sent to Caesarea and from there to Tarsus (see comments on 1:16–18). Evangelization of Syria and Cilicia was after the visit of Galatians 1:18. It seems it could well have been a preaching mission he carried on while he was headquartering at Tarsus (Acts 9:30) and before Barnabas came (Acts 11:25) to get Paul to help him at Antioch. There are others, however, who would treat the chronology differently. The best thing for one to do is study carefully the accounts in Acts and come to his own conclusion. Paul's purpose here is to emphasize that the places where he preached were far from Jerusalem and thus removed from the influence of the other apostles. All of this strengthens Paul's contention that he came to his gospel independently of the other leaders because his revelation was directly from Christ.

1:22—Unknown by face unto the churches of Judea: A better translation might be, "unknown personally." Paul probably means the churches outside of Jerusalem which were in the province of Judea. We would say the rural congregations. Paul had preached in Jerusalem itself. Also, he had earlier been a persecutor. If the traditional description of Paul is accurate, he would be a hard man to forget. He has been pictured as a short, baldheaded man with bushy eyebrows and piercing eyes. He is also supposed to have been bowlegged.

1:23—Teacheth the faith which once he destroyed: The use of faith as a noun gives it an objective sense. This makes it synonymous with "the gospel" as in Acts 6:7; 13:8. Surely one who had heard Paul preach the gospel in those early years would be so impressed that he would spread the word to others. His sharp, stern sentences must have been like the roll of artillery that ushers in the battle. With his rich Old Testament background as a base and his new Christian experience as the dynamic, Paul stirred up people wherever he went. His name had become an institution. This one who had formerly sought to destroy the Christian faith was now trying just as hard (perhaps even harder) to build it up.

1:24—They glorified God in me: This is not "through me" but rather "in me" which some have translated "in my case." The history, words, and deeds of the apostle gave reassurance and, therefore, cause for rejoicing to all of the followers of Christ in the churches of Judea. This is a further verification of Paul's argument in this chapter. The people recognized his gospel and accorded him full status and recognition. What Peter and James did later, the country churches of Judea did earlier. They granted Paul status. They regarded him as a true convert and as a sincere Christian and received him as a bona fide preacher of the gospel of Christ. It was not so much that they marveled at him nor that they praised him or were struck with admiration. It was rather that they recognized that the grace of God was operative in his life both in his conversion experience and in his effective proclamation of the gospel.

6.   A Much Later Visit and Its Results (2:1–10)

2:1—Fourteen years after: Scholars are disagreed on the date from which the fourteen years is to be reckoned. The most obvious is, of course, the one mentioned in 1:18. Some commentators, on the other hand, would date this from his initial conversion experience.

I went up again to Jerusalem: Luke mentions five visits of Paul to Jerusalem (Acts 9:26; 11:30; 15:1; 18:22; 21:15). It seems safe to say that scholarship is virtually unanimous in identifying this visit with the great Jerusalem Conference recorded in Acts 15. There is agreement in so many of the chief points that the evidence seems overwhelming. Perhaps the only real difficulty lies in the fact that the writer of Acts makes this the *third* visit of Paul to Jerusalem after his conversion experience but the book of Galatians would seem to indicate that it was only the *second*. The fact is, however, that Paul is not attempting, in the book of Galatians, to outline all of the visits. He is mentioning only those that might have any bearing upon his relationship with the apostles concerning doctrine.

With Barnabas, and took Titus with me also: There is a difference in Paul's relationship with Barnabas and with Titus. Barnabas was Paul's colleague. The church at Antioch had commissioned the two equally for the missionary journey. Titus was one of those referred to in Acts 15:2 as "certain other of them" and was taken by Paul, no doubt, for a specific reason. He was a Gentile and would become a "test-case" for the disputed matter. Paul assumes in the letter that the Galatians are familiar with Titus. He may have been, by the time of the writing of the letter, a fellow traveler and certainly a trusted helper of Paul.

Paul felt he had an irrefutable argument for his side of the case when he took with him an uncircumcised Gentile who had become a Christian and evidenced every qualification of being a follower of Christ. Paul wanted to do more than show his Christian liberty. He wanted to furnish an example which would forever shut the mouths of his enemies concerning whether or not noncircumcised people could receive the full privileges of being a Christian. This was a case in point which was important to Paul because it proved his contention conclusively. He intended to push this argument for all it was worth. When he showed that Titus could be as good a Christian as the Jews, Paul knew the arguments the Judaizers presented for perpetuating separatism would fall of their own weight. The way would then be open for the Spirit of God to bind all Christians into one great fellowship.

2:2—Went up by revelation: This was an important moment in Paul's life. The question was a critical one. Paul looked for and received direct guidance from God. George Findlay says, "Never had he more urgently needed or more implicitly relied upon divine direction than at this hour." There is no contradiction between Paul's statement and the record in Acts 15:2 that it was a decision of the church that he and the others should go up to Jerusalem. There is no reason to doubt that Paul received a direct revelation concerning his mission. He was not going in order to *seek* instruction from the apostles. He was not dependent upon them. He went to advise with them, and he was under the influence of a direct revelation from God. He wished to show—what he thought God wanted them to know—that he was as much under divine commission as any of them.

But privately to them which were of reputation: The Greek word for "them which were of reputation" is the plural participle from the word which means to seem or to appear. A literal translation would be "to the seeming ones" or "the appearing ones"; that is, those who "seem to be." This would be the ones mentioned in 2:9—James, Cephas, and John. In verse 9 he speaks of them as those "who seem to be pillars." Paul's independence is clearly reflected in every statement he makes. He does not recognize anyone as superior to himself. He is equal in every sense of the word to those who are the accepted leaders in Christendom of that day.

Those who do not agree that this visit is the same as in Acts 15:2 argue that there is no place in the account in Acts for a private meeting. A closer reading, however, shows that Acts 15:6 speaks of a separate meeting that some of the leaders had in order to work out the problems before coming back to the larger audience. This was good common sense and Paul always sought to be reasonable in every matter requiring wise judgment.

I should run or had run, in vain: Although the verb "run" was used of a messenger in carrying news of a victory, Paul uses it here, as in several other places (1 Cor. 9:24–26; Phil. 2:16; Gal. 5:7), in a moral sense. It is significant that Paul does not speak of his concern that there might be a rift in Christian fellowship. He is anxious rather that the truth of the gospel message might not be compromised. If he failed to convince the others of the validity of the message he preached, the work among the Gentiles would be hindered. Paul was not nearly as concerned with some kind of superficial unity among the brethren as he was in establishing clearly the truth he preached, which he was certain had come by special revelation from God. Paul was convinced he had not changed ground. Those who opposed him had moved. This was especially important in view of the fact that the Judaizers were constantly accusing him of being a "shifty fellow, always adapting his gospel to his hearers." Paul had performed his work eagerly and strenuously. He had no intention of compromising his message; but he was concerned with the proposal of the Judaizers which, if adopted, would be tantamount to obliterating all that he had accomplished with so much hard work.

2:3—Neither Titus . . . being a Greek was compelled to be circumcised: The traditional interpretation of this verse is that Paul held out and would not have Titus circumcised. He had become a Christian without circumcision. If it had been necessary to be circumcised in order to become a Christian, Titus would have been circumcised earlier. When Paul came to Jerusalem there were those who insisted, but Paul would not give in for even a brief period of time to them. This noble specimen of evangelization among the Gentiles was Paul's pride and joy. This "case in point" must be allowed to stand.

There was a difference between Titus and Timothy. In Acts 16:3 Paul agreed to Timothy's circumcision because Timothy was half Jew. His mother was a Jewess but his father was a Greek. Paul did not have Timothy circumcised in order for him to become a Christian. He agreed to it in order to please the Jews who placed a high value on circumcision as a Jewish custom. Timothy was probably quite willing to accept a ceremony which normally would have been performed on him in childhood. With Titus, however, it was different. To Paul, it was a matter of principle. When the Judaizers insisted upon it, Paul insisted just as strongly against it.

But all scholars have not agreed with this traditional interpretation. The difficulty begins with a textual problem in verse 5. Some of the early manuscripts omit the Greek words *hois oude* which is translated in English by "to whom" and "no, not." In other words, verse 5 would read "We gave place by subjection for an hour" (the Greek word for hour means a brief period of time). When this fact is viewed in light of verse 3, the possible, and perhaps probable, meaning of verse 3 is that Titus was circumcised but the action did not come *because of compulsion.* Scholars who take this position claim that Paul agreed to the circumcision of Titus as a gesture but did not regard it as compromising a principle. *The New English Bible* has a marginal reading which says that Titus "was under no absolute compulsion to be circumcised, but for the sake of certain . . . I yielded to their demand for the moment, to ensure that gospel truth should not be prevented from reaching you." In order to build this case, some scholars point out that in Galatians 5:11 Paul defends himself from the accusation of still preaching circumcision.

Moffatt claims that some of the phrases which Paul uses, coupled with the passionate vindication of his independence throughout the book as a whole, suggests he had given his opponents some kind of "handle" for their claim that he accepted some form of "subjection." Moffatt claims some concession must have been made by Paul, and he contends the only likely occasion would have been on this trip to Jerusalem. It has also been claimed that the very incoherence of the language argues in favor of this contention. If Paul had absolutely refused the circumcision of Titus and the others had agreed, Paul would certainly have stated it very strongly and pointed out that they had completely yielded to his side. The language, however, is vague and this complete syntax of verses 3–5 seems to indicate that Paul is not expressing himself as clearly and forcefully as he usually does but is indulging in some kind of avoidance of the issue. These scholars claim that it is clear Paul made some kind of compromise, and they suggest that in a moment of weakness or in a moment of "unclear thinking" he agreed to circumcise Titus as a gesture but later regretted that he did.

What kind of conclusion can we arrive at concerning the question? First, we must realize that the strongest argument for this latter position rests upon a textual change. It would be necessary then to make a thorough study in textual criticism. It must be admitted that verses 3–5 are difficult. Paul is obviously emotionally excited and this leads him into involved grammar and unfinished sentences. Something seems to have happened to upset Paul. It could be that Titus was circumcised, but most students of Paul somehow cannot believe that Paul yielded even in a moment of weakness or mistaken judgment for the sake of expediency. On the other hand, Paul does seem to be defending himself against something which happened.

Alan Cole has given us an interesting interpretation which makes good sense. He suggests that perhaps Paul agreed to the circumcision of Titus. He felt this gesture would be helpful in his debate with the Judaizers. Later, however, before the act was carried out, Paul realized this was an unwise decision. Therefore, he refused permission, and as he looked back at what he did, "his anger boiled over at the treachery of those who led him to take such a step." The Judaizers considered this as "bad faith" and accused Paul of inconsistency. This suggestion of Cole's could apply whether we leave the two disputed Greek words in verse 5 or whether we eliminate them. In other words, we could translate verse 5 "I yielded for the moment" or "I did not yield for a moment" and the ultimate interpretation of the entire passage (vv. 3–5) would be the same. *Titus was not circumcised.*

2:4—False brethren . . . who came in privily to spy out our liberty: Paul challenges the right of these people even to be considered as members of the Christian body. They pretend to be brothers in the Lord. They were received as true Christians, and this gave them the right to speak in the fellowship. The figure in the Greek word is that of a spy who infiltrates the enemy camp and plays the part of one friendly to the cause. In this way he learns the strategic situation of the opposition. As we seek to determine in our own mind whether or not they were Christians, we should realize that Paul calls them "false brethren," and this assumes that he rejected them as being true converts. They must have been similar to the Pharisees who gave Jesus so much trouble during his earthly ministry. They were legalists—of this there is no doubt.

There is certainly much legalism even among Christians of the twentieth century. There must be a question of "sweet reasonableness" in making a judgment as to whether one who possesses a legalistic approach in ethics and morals is truly a born-again Christian. The mature Christian is certainly one who has risen above legalism to spiritual fellowship with Christ that brings liberty in all things. On the other hand, we must be slow to condemn any who have strong convictions concerning certain actions and deeds as legalists. The Christian must keep firm a sense of right and wrong in moral and ethical matters. On the other hand, we must be careful that our evaluation of "right and wrong" is not a projection of our own likes and dislikes rather than a reflection of the spirit of Christ.

The important thing is that these "false brethren," rather than confessing their own sins and asking for God to save them by his grace, came in to bear testimony to the "heresy" of Paul. It is a dangerous time when we become judgmental of others. A truly Christlike person is intolerant of his own sins but very tolerant of the weaknesses of others. As Christians, we should be slow to judge another's motives. Freedom in Christ does not mean license but it does mean liberty. We should recognize the liberty of each person and be slow to condemn him when we do not know all the facts of his life.

2:5—An hour (see comment on v. 3): This Greek word means "a limited portion of time." It is also used in the sense of "a short period" or "an eventful season." The meaning here is certainly not a sixty-minute hour as we know it. Both the RSV and NEB translate it "moment."

2:6—These who seem to be somewhat: Actually, Paul does not finish his sentence. This phrase is what grammarians call an "anacoluthon." Paul probably intended to conclude the sentence by saying that he received nothing from them. In the midst of his excitement, however, he started a parenthetical clause and never went back to finish the sentence. Three times in this book (2:2, 6,9) the phrase *hoi dokuntes* is used. But each time it gains in intensity. In 2:2 Paul is rather courteous but his indignation continues to rise. By the time he reaches verse 9 he drops the vagueness and calls them by name—Peter, James, and John.

Whatsoever they were, it maketh no matter to me: There are two possible suggestions here. Paul may mean "whatever you might like to call them" and be referring to the title of "apostle" or even "pillar" as he refers to them in verse 9. On the other hand, he could be making reference to the fact that they had a privileged opportunity in associating with Jesus during the days of his earthly ministry. If one thinks Paul is speaking a little harshly and with a trace of envy, he should remember that he felt the issue was a great one. His experience had been unusual—even catastrophic.

Quite often today we see one who has had a dynamic and revolutionary change become a bit intolerant of Christians who have settled down to a more stable type ministry and do not seem to preach with the urgency of the new convert. Paul was not infallible. He was a human being, possessed of a great experience with Christ. He was zealous and to some seemed a bit overbearing. It is not fair to call him "anti-establishment" because he always respected authority. He did feel, however, in this case that the apostles needed to be shaken out of their lethargy and understand that the gospel must be completely free of Jewish shackles if it was to be effective in the Gentile world.

Added nothing to me: This is what Paul meant to say in the first place before the parenthesis "got in the way." This phrase is another evidence of his independence. He added nothing to them at his conversion, and they did not add anything to him at this conference. He received his theology directly from God, including, of course, a proper interpretation of the Old Testament.

2:7—To me . . . unto Peter: It was not, of course, Paul who first preached to the Gentiles. Peter had been taught a great lesson (Acts 10:1—11:18) at the home of Cornelius. At the Jerusalem

Conference, Peter was quick to point this out to the brethren (Acts 15:7). James also referred to it (Acts 15:14) in his speech at the Conference. Nevertheless, Paul never considered Peter as one sent especially to the Gentile world.

2:8—He that wrought: Although Paul and Peter had two separate spheres for their major activity, the same God was working through both of them. There were not two different gospels preached to two different classes of people. It was merely that God had defined the spheres of their work. Neither does it mean that Paul preached to Gentiles only nor Peter to Jews only. Each preached to both, but each majored on the area that was assigned to him for his particular emphasis.

2:9—James, Cephas, and John, who seemed to be pillars: Note the material on 2:2 concerning "them which were of reputation" and also in 2:6 concerning "whatsoever they were it maketh no matter to me." Although Paul did not agree that these men were infallible authoritarians, he did feel that he needed the countenance of these men in order to prove to the churches of Galatia that he had the right to regard himself as an apostle. Paul could be a rugged individualist at times, and yet he had the sanctified common sense to recognize his need to work with others in order to be assured of the most effective results. It is interesting that the "Peter, James, and John" combination of Jesus' day continues but with a different "James" since the original one was martyred and the half brother of Jesus became a believer.

The right hands of fellowship: This was a noble action and, no doubt, made an arresting picture. Paul must have exulted in spirit as he recited the event. This public manifestation of their agreement meant that all recognized they were partners and fellow-workers. The handclasp was the seal which indicated there was one gospel and all were colaborers. The clasped right hands signified friendship and mutual confidence in each other. The record does not say whether this handshaking took place publicly so that all the church could witness it or whether it was merely among the leaders in council. Many scholars believe it was before the assembled church so that as many as possible might witness their unity.

We should go unto the heathen . . . they unto the circumcision: The "heathen" represents the Gentiles and the "circumcision" represents the Jews. Literally, heathen means nations. This would be, to the Jews, someone other than their own people. A delightful harmony now existed as the matter was settled. Harsh contention and strife had been avoided. Jealousies were eliminated. Paul was allowed to make a full statement of his opinions. This had been done in private, and the people had been completely satisfied that God had called Paul and Barnabas to work with the Gentiles. Paul had come to Jerusalem to secure this decision. His strongest argument was the fact that Gentiles had been converted. If one is intellectually and spiritually honest, he must accept evidence as it is presented. If the brethren at Jerusalem had closed their eyes to the actual conversion of the Gentiles, they would have come dangerously close to sinning against the Holy Spirit. The "pillars" would never be guilty of such an action. It may be that some of the Judaizers were.

This incident certainly gives us a striking illustration of how to avoid strife. There should be perfect frankness, accompanied by willingness to understand and describe things exactly as they are. Each should be willing to rejoice in the talents, energetic zeal, and spiritual success of someone else even if it causes his own to look small. What a difference could occur in our organized religious life today if all people were willing to display the same firm conviction and yet sweet spirit as these early Christian leaders.

2:10—Should remember the poor . . . which I also was forward to do: The tense of the verb indicates that they were already remembering the poor but were requested to "continue" to do so. The word translated "was forward" conveys the idea of urgency, earnestness, and diligence. The verb is translated various ways—to hasten, to be in earnest about, be bent upon, and to endeavor earnestly. Paul's Jewish background would lead him to follow this request naturally. The Pharisees believed the world stood on three pillars—almsgiving, study of the Torah, and the Temple service. Palestine's economic situation made it necessary to place great emphasis upon this righteous activity of helping the poor. The resources were limited and there was perpetual warfare and political strife. Many people existed on the ragged edge of starvation. The early Christian preachers faced this fact immediately. Man cannot live without bread. The gospel found its most receptive hearers among the underprivileged people. One of the

most honorable titles for the early Christians was "the beggars"—
people at their wit's end both materially and spiritually. It was
impossible to separate preaching the gospel of Christ from helping
those who were poor.

Paul recognized this fact and, in his missionary journeys, he used
the offering for the poor as a way of breaking down the prejudice
of the Jews against the Gentiles. He was convinced that the love
of Christ could reconcile people to each other. One of the most
practical ways of seeing this come to pass was to get them working
on a common task. He believed a profession of faith in Christ must
produce fruit. He refused to allow his converts to have easy comfort with no challenge. What Paul learned as a Jew, because of the
overtilled and overpopulated land of Palestine crammed with
hungry and unproductive mouths, he was already eager to practice among the Gentiles. *The New English Bible* translates, concerning the remembering of the poor, "which was the very thing
I made it my business to do" with a marginal reading "had made"
or "have made" indicating that Paul was eager to continue the
thing which he had already been practicing.

7. Paul's Clash with Peter at Antioch (2:11–14)

2:11—When Peter was come to Antioch: It is not possible for
us to know when this incident occurred. It seems unlikely that
Peter would have been this inconsistent after the Jerusalem Conference. The most logical time would have been during the period
that Saul and Barnabas were laboring together at Antioch before
they were set aside by the church for special missionary activity.
We are not told how long the totality of their ministry was during
that period. We are told that they "assembled themselves with the
church, and taught much people" for a whole year (Acts 11:26).
We are also told that they made a trip to Jerusalem to carry relief
to those who were in need (Acts 11:29–30). We are not told how
long they continued to labor in the church at Antioch after they
returned from the trip to Jerusalem and before they were set aside
and sent on their first missionary journey (Acts 13:1–3). The verb
"was come" can be translated "had come" (it actually means
"came"), and this would indicate Peter had been there for a
lengthy time when the incident occurred. It does seem necessary
for him to have been in Antioch long enough for people to realize

he had no objection to eating with the Gentiles. All in all, the "period of one year" (Acts 11:26) seems to be the most logical time.

I withstood him to the face: We need to remember that, although Peter and Paul were great interpreters of Christ, they were human beings. They did not always agree and sometimes their disagreements became intense. Paul was independent and never failed to speak openly and with courage concerning his convictions. Peter had been considered the leader of the Christians—a path breaker in the work of evangelism. He was highly esteemed by his brethren. It was not easy to oppose him face to face, but Paul felt this issue was important enough that Peter's inconsistency must be pointed out publicly. This was not a mere "personality clash" but was rather a debate of an issue that must be settled early in order to prevent disastrous results.

He was to be blamed: Early in the history of Christianity, Roman Catholic students saw a threat to Peter's authority in the church by this statement of Paul. It militated strongly against Peter's infallibility as "head of the church" and the first pope of the Roman Church. Some commentators sought to remove the difficulty by coming to the conclusion that this was not Simon Peter but one of the seventy. Other scholars contended this disputation took place because of a prearrangement among the apostles. Herman Ridderbos calls such interpretations "sheer hypotheses" and maintains they cannot be accepted. Martin Luther also made much of Paul's public resistance to Peter. There has been a school of thought for many centuries concerning the unreconcilable conflict between Peter and Paul but this seems to be overemphasized. They were not opponents. They had an honest difference of opinion. Paul did not feel the necessity to compromise with the Palestinian Jews in any way. He was a Jew of Tarsus. He had been commissioned to the Gentile world and he felt no obligation to "play politics" or seek in any way to protect the feelings of people whom he felt were narrow and bigoted and failing in worldwide vision.

2:12—Certain came from James: This is plural (meaning certain ones) but some manuscripts indicate only one. These were "men from James," who was recognized as the leader of the church at Jerusalem. Their position was not that of those who have been mentioned in this letter. They had not come to condemn the

preaching of the gospel to Gentiles nor had they come to demand
that the Gentile converts be circumcised. Their purpose was to
remind the Jewish Christians in Antioch of the obligation which
Jews (and they insisted this meant Jewish-Christians also) must
bear in mind in their social relationships with Gentiles.

Did eat with the Gentiles: The Pentateuch did not absolutely
forbid eating with the Gentiles. This tradition had grown up during the days of Antiochus Epiphanes when the Jews separated
themselves in order to avoid the growing menace of Greek customs. Good Jews were required to keep themselves scrupulously
apart from non-Jews. They were to do more than merely observe
their own regulations concerning diet, methods of cooking, wash-
ing of plates, etc.; they were to refuse to even sit down with
Gentiles at the same table. There were probably various opinions
concerning how strictly this practice should be enforced. It may
be that some Jews were willing to allow the Gentiles to come to
their table since the rules about food could be observed there. A
strict Jew would, however, because of his fear of pollution, never
accept an invitation to dine with a Gentile. A further point that
aggravated the situation was that it was a common practice among
the Gentiles to eat meat bought in the marketplace which had first
been offered to a pagan deity. Paul, of course, dealt with this latter
subject in his letter to the Corinthians.

What was the true Christian attitude? The Jew who had accepted Christ as fulfilment of the messianic hope was still a Jew
and could not be disloyal to his traditions. He could not ignore
anything which he felt degraded the ethical and religious standards of Judaism. His Christian love might lead him to accept an
invitation from a Gentile Christian, but some thought there was
a real danger in being led to eat food which they, as Jews, felt was
unclean. These Jews may have felt that if they ignored the Jewish
laws, they would forfeit or at least seriously hurt their chance of
winning their fellow Israelites to accept the gospel.

**2:12—When they were come, he withdrew and separated him-
self:** Peter must have had mingled emotions. It is only fair that we
give him credit for proper motivation. He had already shown a
big Christian spirit in his attitude toward Cornelius who was a
Gentile. In his heart, Peter was ready to fraternize with the Gentile Christians. He had generous sympathies and true Christian

love from the outset. It seems that he felt he had gone further than his good judgment should have taken him. When the group came from Jerusalem, he seems to have panicked and in a moment of weak vacillation made a compromise that harmed the cause of Christ with the Gentiles more than it could possibly have helped it with the Jews. Moffatt says, "The situation was too involved for him to know what was right and what was wrong. His dishonor was rooted in honor."

2:13—The other Jews dissembled likewise . . . Barnabas also was carried away: Peter was a strong personality. When he rushed into the resurrection tomb, the other disciple who had outrun him "went in also" (John 20:4,8). Here, even Barnabas, the steady, trusted colaborer of Paul, was carried away and separated himself from the Jews—probably against his better judgment.

2:14—When I saw that they walked not uprightly according to the truth of the gospel: A literal translation says, "were not straight footing toward the gospel." Paul recognized they were pulling farther and farther away from the true principles of the gospel. It is not that Paul was a legalist, but he did recognize that there were certain guidelines which must be observed in order to present the gospel message in its purity.

I said unto Peter before them all: Paul spoke directly to Peter because he felt the matter was urgent enough to bring it out into the open. The rest of the Jews were equally guilty. He did not, however, feel that it was practical to visit each one separately; but by rebuking Peter publicly he was, in reality, speaking a word to all of them. In John Calvin's commentary on this verse he says, "This example instructs us that those who have sinned publicly must be publicly chastised, as far as the church is concerned. The purpose is that their sin may not, by remaining unpunished, form a dangerous example." If this seems harsh, we should remember that Paul says virtually the same thing in his first letter to Timothy (5:20), "Them that sin rebuke before all, that others also may fear."

Thou, being a Jew, livest after the manner of Gentiles: It seems to have been common knowledge in the church at Antioch that Peter had begun to live like a "non-Jew." He had been the recipient of a unique revelation from God in the case of Cornelius. The church at Jerusalem had accepted his report of the indident.

Why compellest thou the Gentiles to live as do the Jews: Paul's contention was that Peter was inconsistent. He had taken his stand concerning the conversion of Gentiles. He had accepted them on the same level with the Jews and had gone so far as to fellowship with them in meals. The implication of this acceptance was that faith in Christ made all believers one. Either Peter was wrong in accepting the Gentiles, or he was wrong in retrogressing and refusing to associate with them in the eating of meals when the group from Jerusalem came and put pressure upon him. Paul may have been strongly influenced by the fact that Jesus ate with publicans and sinners who were considered unclean. Surely, however, his chief motive was that he did not want a division to come into the churches that would hinder the work of preaching the gospel to the Gentile world. He recognized that either the Jewish Christians must transcend the legal restrictions of Judaism in favor of the larger Christian fellowship or else the Gentile Christians must become Jews. Peter, being sympathetic originally to the first, was now, according to Paul, falling backward by acquiescing to the second. He was virtually forcing the Gentiles to become Jews.

8. Paul's Theological Position (2:15–21)

2:15—Jews by nature . . . not sinners of the Gentiles: There is a question as to whether verses 15–17 represent words that Paul spoke to Peter or whether they are words he is writing to the Galatians. It seems more logical that this represents a continuation of Paul's dialogue with Peter since he emphasizes the superiority of the natural Jew. Paul and Peter would agree that the Jews were highly privileged in contradistinction to the Gentiles who were considered coarse sinners by physical Israel.

2:16—Man is not justified by the works of the law: Paul had come a long way in his religious experience. In another letter he described his pre-Christian life as "touching the righteousness which is in the law, blameless" (Phil. 3:6). Now, he is just as certain that no keeping of the law can pile up merit to provide a righteous standing before God. We come to a new appreciation for others when we realize it is not our good works which bring us into a righteous relationship with God. Our self-esteem vanishes. We cease to look down upon others. If one believes strict obedience to legal requirements will bring him into favor with God, he will be self-righteous and will seek to impose this legalism upon others.

Actually, nobody has ever been justified by law because nobody has ever kept the law perfectly. We may keep some of the law's demands, but no one except Jesus has ever fulfilled all the law in his life. John Stott says, "The astonishing thing is that anybody has ever imagined he could get to God and to Heaven that way."

Justified by the faith of Christ: Paul's concept of justification is almost always in the forensic sense. William Hendriksen defines it as "that gracious act of God whereby, on the basis solely of Christ's accomplished mediatorial work, he declares the sinner just, and the latter accepts this benefit with a believing heart." It is charging the sinner's guilt to Christ. The righteousness of Christ is imputed to the sinner. Justification is a "once for all" verdict. Man is justified only once—when he receives Christ as Savior and comes into a new standing with God. Man cannot earn this justification. He can only accept it as God's free gift.

This verse, of course, does not tell the full story about the salvation experience. Justification is accompanied by regeneration or the new birth. Man is justified when he repents of sin and places his faith in Christ as a Savior. The Holy Spirit comes into his heart and transformation takes place. The experience of justification is never a reality unless it is accompanied by the regenerating power of the Holy Spirit. Paul here, however, is emphasizing the justification experience and insisting that it does not come by "piling up good works" in an effort to obligate God to justify man. The phrase "by the faith of Christ" does not mean by Christ's faith but by our faith in Christ. A technical study of the Greek prepositions convinces us that Paul was one of the greatest grammarians as well as logicians who ever lived. F. B. Meyer is reported to have said that after a thorough study of the Greek New Testament he was convinced that even the prepositions were inspired by God.

2:17—Is therefore Christ the minister of sin?: There are those who interpret this verse similarly to Romans 6:1 ff. and see a direct reference to the charge that Paul was preaching "antinomianism." Those who held this view contended salvation by grace through faith alone removed all incentive for righteous living and would lead to a lower moral standard than under the law of Moses. This would make Christ a "minister of sin." There is an element of correctness in believing Paul was answering the charge of antinomianism here, but there is something more. The heart of

Paul's gospel was that all men are equal sinners before God. He seeks to present this as sympathetically as possible from the standpoint of those who were born Jews. Those who valued Jewish privilege and background believed that all men were not equally sinners in God's sight. They valued the privileges of Jewish heritage with its much higher moral standards than the pagan Gentiles. Those who were steeped in Jewish legalism felt Peter and Paul forgot the Jewish heritage when they ranked themselves before God as no better than the Gentiles. The Jew was not thinking merely of ceremonial or legal righteousness but was referring to the low standards of morality in the Gentile world. He was profoundly concerned lest fraternization with the Gentiles would reduce the Jew to their level. When one thus misinterpreted Paul's position, he could say that faith in Christ took good Jews and made them sinners like the Gentiles.

God forbid: Paul's first reaction was an indignant repudiation. The expression is a strong one—one of the strongest possible in the language. It is found again in 3:21 and no fewer than ten times in Romans. It is his customary expression to demolish an argument which sounds logical from a human standpoint but which, if accepted, is wholly incompatible with the known character and purposes of God. Paul was intolerant of human wisdom which ignored the truth of revealed religion.

2:18—Build again the things which I destroyed: Paul is very tactful as he switches to the first person singular. The thing he speaks of in this verse is exactly that of which Peter was guilty. By his example, Peter was reestablishing legalistic religion which he had previously destroyed in insisting that Christians were justified from the law of Moses. The law had one purpose—to show men they were sinners and needed a Savior. Those who turned back to works of the law in order to secure life vitiated the very nature and purpose of the law. Paul felt very strongly concerning those who unwittingly reestablished what they had previously so wisely torn down. It should be borne in mind that Paul is still speaking of his conversation with Peter, but the implications of his contention apply to the Galatians as well who were in danger of going back to a legalistic approach rather than remaining with faith in Christ as the basis of their relationship to God.

2:19—Dead to the law, that I might live unto God: Paul no longer considered the law of Moses as a means of being justified. In this sense, he acted as though it did not exist. It exerted no influence on him and thus he was as insensible to it as a dead man is to things around him. It was no longer his grand aim and purpose in life. What about the phrase "through the law" which precedes? Some have interpreted this as meaning "the law of the Spirit of life in Christ Jesus" which Paul uses in Romans 8:2 as a description of the Christian life. In other words, Paul is living within the sphere of a new law because of a new relationship and this makes him dead to the old law. Other scholars, however, believe Paul means that by understanding the true nature of the law of Moses he had become dead to it. He had ceased to expect any justification through this law. He understood the extent of its requirements but came to understand its limitations. While he had not fully understood its nature, it had been the entire object of his life because he felt he could be saved by it. His experience with Christ, however, brought him face to face with the folly of trusting the law. He was now "dead" to it as a means of justification. This does not, of course, mean that he did not appreciate the moral values within it. He is speaking here, however, of its uselessness as a basis of securing a right standing before God.

2:20—Crucified with Christ: Paul was not willing to cherish any belief nor accept any maxim unless it was rooted and grounded in the death of Christ. His world of Judaism and personal pride died when he surrendered to Jesus. Paul's fundamental concept of God was grace, but the death of Christ was the fundamental way in which God's grace manifested itself. Thus, the center of Paul's theology was the crucifixion. The stumbling block of Judaism was the refusal to accept a *crucified* Messiah. The idea was revolting that the messianic hope of Israel culminated in the crucifixion. Once, however, Paul understood the true meaning of the crucifixion and experienced the resurrected Christ, his whole world changed. Just as surely as Christ died on the cross, Paul died to his dependence on the legalistic system of Judaism as his hope. He was nailed to the cross of legalism and died to the complete system.

Nevertheless I live . . . Christ liveth in me: If we were to attempt a one-phrase summary of Paul's basic religious concept it would be "union with Christ." This was the heartbeat of his mes-

sage. James Stewart said, "If one seeks for the most characteristic
sentences the apostle ever wrote, they will be found, not where
he is refuting the legalists, or vindicating his apostleship, or meditating on eschatological hopes, or giving practical ethical guidance
to the Church, but where his intense intimacy with Christ comes
to expression." The new environment of the redeemed man is the
presence of Christ. Man is no longer living within the cramping
restrictions of the old life. He is in an entirely different sphere—
the sphere of Christ. In the new birth he was transplanted into
new soil and a new climate. His redeemed spirit is breathing in
a new and nobler element.

W. W. McGregor once said, "Just as a bird lives in the air and
needs the air to live in, just as a fish lives in the water and can live
nowhere else, so, in Paul's view, a Christian man requires the
presence of his Master." If man's faith in God is to grow, it must
be rooted in the awareness of Christ as a living contemporary. We
cannot maintain a living faith in Christ if he is but a childish
recollection. The God we know in a present-tense experience
through Jesus Christ is the God we will never outgrow. Paul's old
life in the flesh had given place to a new life. It was one in which
Christ had taken complete possession of him. The redemptive
work of Christ breaks through into the life of the believer in such
a way that Christ lives in him. Some theologians have spoken of
this as the "continuing incarnation."

2:21—Do not frustrate the grace of God: The verb means literally "displace," "set aside," or "abrogate." To Paul, the grace of
God was responsible for everything he was. He expressed it quite
succinctly, "by the grace of God I am what I am" (1 Cor. 15:10).
Paul would do nothing to make void or render null this marvelous
grace. He would pursue no course that even minimized God's
grace. He would permit nothing in his life or conduct which would
even suggest grace had no influence over one's heart and life. It
was the grace of God that had arrested him and turned him about
from his wild and fanatical career of persecution. The law had left
him in bondage but the grace of God had set him free. He could
speak of it only in the most glowing terms of appreciation.

If righteousness . . . by the law, then Christ is dead in vain: The
grace of God and the death of Christ on the cross are wedded
together in an undissoluble amalgamation in Paul's writings. The

death of Christ was more than that of a martyr. The average newspaper reporter of that day might have told the story in a few paragraphs, but one who had come face to face with the redemptive work of God in Christ could never exhaust the depth of its meaning. Man and God transact their most important business at Calvary. Man finds there his righteousness and nowhere else is it available. If man can find a right standing before God through performing the perfunctories of legal obedience, the death of Christ was the most cruel and senseless event in the history of the world.

We can never explain fully the depth of the atonement. If the cross were not too broad for human comprehension, it would be too narrow to meet human need. But God felt it was necessary! Calvary was the climax of that which began in Bethlehem. It is the supreme personal event of history where God and man meet on the deepest possible level. God comes to grips with all of the elements which separate his creation from him. It is at the cross that men are drawn near and placed in a new relationship with God. It is not man holding on to God but God, through Christ, grasping man and holding him. It is through the death of Christ that God's hand of grace reaches through to sinful man. The performance of the law and its requirements could never do what the death of Christ on Calvary did. Paul has made his choice as the grounds of justification. It is Calvary—and he will glory in it and sing its praises forever.

II. The Heart of Paul's Message
3:1 to 4:31

Paul has finished his formal defense of his apostleship by an appeal to his own commission from the Lord. He is now ready to refute the objections of the Judaizers and set forth a clear statement of the doctrine he preaches. This section deals to a large extent with an appeal to the Old Testament Scriptures for vindication of Paul's message.

After a brief appeal to the Galatians upon a personal basis, Paul gives an extended explanation of justification by faith based upon Abraham's obedience and shows this was, in reality, a foreshadowing of the gospel. The law did come in for a brief period but it was not to replace the promise made to Abraham. It served an interim function but was never equal, much less superior, to the covenant made with Abraham.

Those who are in Christ, Paul insists, are the true children of God and have received the promises made to Abraham. The law was a help in making men realize their need for salvation, but it neither supplied nor kept in force the relationship to God that is entered and maintained only by faith in Christ.

The new spiritual life means an end to slavery. The condition of those under the law was similar to that of an heir placed under a guardian for a fixed time. God set the conditions and the time for the great liberation. Those who have thus been set free should never permit themselves to be enslaved again by falling into the pattern of life of their pre-Christian days. Paul once more appeals to them personally before giving another exposition of Scripture based upon the life of Abraham.

These two chapters have one dominant theme—Christ has come that we may be free. God wishes the best for his people. He desires for them liberty—not enslavement to a hopelessly impossible set of rules. Only this type of life can be the victorious one.

1. A Personal Appeal (3:1–5)

3:1—O foolish Galatians: The word "foolish" has been variously translated. Paul is not reprimanding them for lack of intellectual understanding but rather their lack of spiritual insight. Luke uses this same Greek word where he records Jesus as speaking of those who were "slow of heart to believe" (Luke 24:25). The etymology of the word is interesting. The Greek *anoatos* is derived from the Greek root *noeo* which means to perceive, observe, to mark attentively, to understand, to comprehend, or to conceive. When the alpha is added as a prefix the word is negativized. Thus the word means one who does not perceive, observe, or comprehend. A literal translation would be "O non-comprehending Galatians." This seems much better than "foolish" or "stupid."

Galatians: It is very doubtful that we can draw any conclusion as to the "north and south Galatian theory" by the fact that Paul addresses the people as Galatians. (See discussion in Overview.) Some feel that the fact Paul speaks of them as "Galatians" proves they are Galatians by race and thus must be the people of the northern plateau. There is no reason, however, why the people of the administrative area could not be addressed by the term. There is also no reason for believing Paul is using the word as an epithet of abuse. It is true that in some of the old Hellenistic literature the Galatians are referred to by a Greek word that means stupid, but it is very doubtful that Paul would use such a strong term of offense in order to lead his converts to see his point. Paul addressed them as he did in order to make his letter a bit more personal, hoping to lead them to see his position.

Who hath bewitched you: Paul is not implying that he himself believed in witchcraft, but he does use a word that suggests a deadly fascination similar to that of the "evil eye." There is no doubt Paul believed in a struggle in the spiritual world between powers of righteousness and powers of evil. The New Testament speaks of Satan entering into Judas (Luke 22:3; John 13:27). Paul's verb actually means to mislead by deception as though through the magic arts. It gives the idea of fascinating or influencing by a charm. The point Paul is making is that the Galatians have not been brought to their position by sober reasoning and rational judgment. There has been some evil work among them that has paralyzed their minds. It is similar to the cunning with which the serpent beguiled Eve.

Pointing out that Paul uses the singular "who" rather than the plural, some have concluded that Paul is speaking of one supreme leader among the Judaizers of whose identity Paul was ignorant. From this, they look back to 2:12 and insist the pronoun there should be singular also. This is of doubtful value, however, for the emphasis in this phrase seems to be on the verb rather than on the interrogative pronoun. Paul is not actually interested as to the personal identification of the troublemaker. There may have been one supreme leader but there is nothing to really indicate it and if there were, it is not of great importance. Paul is more interested in getting the Galatians to "think straight" rather than to locate and punish the ringleader of the opposition.

Set forth, crucified among you: The beginning of the Galatians' folly was they had forgotten the cross of Jesus. If they had kept before them the sufferings of the Savior on Calvary, legalism could never have won even a minor victory among them. G. G. Findlay says, "Let the cross of Christ once lose its spell for us, let its influence fail to hold and rule the soul, and we are at the mercy of every wind of doctrine. We are like sailors in a dark flight on a perilous coast, who have lost sight of the lighthouse beacon. Our Christianity will go to pieces." The word for "set forth" has been translated "placarded." Paul seems to be continuing his figure of speech concerning the "eyes" and the suggestion is if they had continued to gaze steadily upon the crucified Messiah they would not have been deceived and become a prey to the evil spell that had misled them. The Greek word suggests a display of something which is of civic interest.

Perhaps the large advertisements that we see on the side of our highways would serve as the best parallel for our contemporary world. Christ had been openly displayed. He had been clearly and publicly proclaimed to the Galatians. They had seen him with their very eyes. The mental picture they had formed of him must have been clear and vivid. They should have continued to meditate upon that which had been announced to them with the upmost clearness. There was no need for them to make a mistake concerning anything which had been so vividly presented to them. Their forgetfulness is inexcusable.

3:2—This only would I learn of you: There is the spirit of reproof in these words. Paul wishes to convince them that when they first embraced Christanity their beliefs were correct. The word "only" implies the argument he is about to present was sufficient for the whole matter if they would but face it candidly and answer it correctly.

Received ye the Holy Spirit: Paul is assuming their true conversion. There was no doubt that the many manifestations which had accompanied their religious experience were legitimately the work of the Holy Spirit. They had been renewed in heart and sanctified in soul. He had comforted the Galatians in their afflictions. He had put his seal on them and demonstrated his presence by signs and wonders among them. The irrefutable testimony of God's presence is always the work of his Spirit. There was no doubting the genuineness of the religious experience of the Galatians.

Works of the law . . . the hearing of faith?: Paul's question was designed to break the enchantment of the Galatians and bring them face to face with reality. What was it that brought joy and peace to the hearts of the Galatians? When were they first conscious of having the Holy Spirit in their hearts? Was it when they submitted to the rigorous bondage of the Jewish ceremonies, or was it when they placed their simple trust in Jesus and received him eagerly in their hearts as Savior? Paul had no doubt that their Christian life had begun in faith. He had no fear of placing the issue before them. He was confident that even a few moments of sober reflection would cause the Galatians to realize it was faith which responded to the marvelous message of Christ and opened the door to God's grace.

There is no virtue in discussing at length whether the "hearing of faith" refers to faith's hearing or to the faith which is heard. It is not of great moment whether faith is the instrument or the accompaniment of hearing. Such minute analysis contributes very little to proper interpretation. Paul is referring to a kind of hearing which believes the gospel, welcomes Christ into the heart, and leads the hearer to surrender himself fully to both the saviorhood and lordship of Christ. When this is done in faith, the Holy Spirit comes into one's life. Perhaps the best metaphor to explain it is that of a new birth. The Galatians had become new creatures not by seeking to obey the traditions handed down from Moses but rather by personally surrendering in faith to the forgiveness Jesus offered and to the new life in him which came through a personal response to his redemptive love.

3:3—Having begun in the spirit: Paul says nothing further concerning the question he asked in verse 2. He assumes the answer is self-evident. He rather chides them for their failure to see the obvious and act upon it. To him, there is no doubt they would agree that their new beginning came through the Spirit. Surely no one of the Galatians would disagree with the fact that one becomes a Christian by a spiritual birth not by a natural or physical one.

Are ye now made perfect by the flesh?: The word for perfect means literally "to bring to completion" or "to finish" rather than the idea of complete sinlessness. Paul's contention is their Christian career started in an experience so pure and exalted that it is not even to be compared with the carnal ordinances of Jewish legalism. Paul considers it inconceivable that they could consider laws and ceremonies as an advance on the relationship which they have come into with Christ by faith. For one to do this, one must forget the spiritual nature of religion and the beautiful simplicity of the blessedness of personal fellowship with Jesus. It is not far from this legalistic approach to an actually worldly-minded practice of life.

3:4—Suffered so many things: The Greek verb used here *(pascho)* is usually translated "suffer." Many scholars, however, feel this verb does not definitely denote adversities but rather experiences. These experiences could be either good or evil. These interpreters thus understand Paul to be referring to the spiritual experiences of the Galatians after their conversion. This is by no means, however, a universally accepted interpretation. The Galatians had, no doubt, suffered many persecutions from their fellow countrymen. If Paul is writing to the churches in South Galatia, there is ample evidence in Acts 14 of how Paul and Barnabas suffered. It is only reasonable to suppose that the converts to Christianity suffered equally.

If it be yet in vain: Paul is assured of better things for his people. The grammatical construction in the original language is such that a loophole is left for doubt and then widened to an unwillingness on the part of the writer to believe that the thing stated will happen. As Paul considers their sufferings, he cannot accept the fact that they have been of no avail. The Galatians have been shaky in their convictions but their faith has not been completely overthrown. There is a reward which comes because of much suffering. Surely the Galatians will reap the harvest of a return to true Christian principles!

3:5—He . . . that ministereth to you the Spirit: The one of whom Paul speaks is God. This thought transcends everything else in his thinking. The reality of God's work among them surpasses in significance everything else. The verb implies liberality. Lightfoot translates, "He that supplieth bountifully" and calls attention to a passage in classical Greek where the word speaks of "the luxuries, the superfluities of the meal." The Greek word for "ministereth" has an interesting history. In its early and shorter form it meant supplying everything the chorus needed in a Greek drama. This kind of giving is more than enough.

Worketh miracles among you: The noun is better translated power, strength, or ability. It has to do with energy and authority. The preposition is probably "in" rather than "among." Thus the passage means "the one working power in you" which fits the context much better. This does not mean that God did not work miracles. There is ample evidence that the early disciples performed many acts which can be explained only by the supernatural even as their Master had done. The thought here, however, is on the influence of the Spirit in the life of the believers giving them power because of their unique relationship with God in Christ. We do not know the exact nature of the powers. It may be that the people were able to exert authority over the physical world as well as the moral world. We should especially note that Paul assumes his converts possess extraordinary powers because of the presence of God's Spirit in their lives. Paul nowhere doubted the genuineness of the religious experience of the Galatians.

Works of the law . . . hearing of faith? Once more this question is urged upon the readers. There is no need to assume a textual problem because of the repetition. The issue was an urgent one and Paul drives it home with all the forceful rhetoric available in his vocabulary. (See comments on v. 2.)

2.   The Gospel and Abraham's Faith (3:6–18)

3:6—Even as: Verse 6 is not so much a subordinate clause, which looks back to and is dependent on verse 5, as it is the introduction of a new topic. The theme which he introduces here continues to the end of chapter 4 and actually sprouts forth anew in chapter 5. The Greek word *kathos* which is translated "even as" is used quite often to introduce a new topic. It is used, more or less, as a text for the exhortation and comments which follow.

Abraham believed God: Paul's enemies have been relying strongly on the Old Testament to prove their case. Therefore, he decides he will meet them on their own grounds. They have made much of Moses. He will carry the argument back further. The righteousness that comes by faith is more ancient than the Mosaic system of laws and ceremonies. In the days of the patriarchs faith was the root of religion. The Jews of Paul's day were proud to be called "Abraham's seed." The bosom of Abraham was heaven to the Israelites. God dealt with Abraham as a righteous man, but Abraham lived many years before the law was given. What was the nature of his righteousness? It was his simple trust. He took God at his word and believed God would perform all he promised.

Accounted to him for righteousness: This was more than "legal fiction." It was a new standing before God. Actually there are only two basic ways by which men seek salvation. They are in direct contrast with each other. One school of thought says man is justified before God by the deeds that he does; while the other says man can offer no merit of his own, but must come in simple faith asking God to have mercy because of his great grace and receive him with forgiving love. The latter is the way of faith. When one approaches God in this manner, he is accepted into the family of God and has all the privileges of sonship.

3:7—The same are the children of Abraham: Paul's enemies were constantly boasting about their descent from Abraham. They seemed to believe this biological circumstance gave them a higher rating with God. Paul's teaching was opposed to their belief but, in reality, it was nothing new. Christ had taught that it was not physical genealogy but spiritual likeness which made one a true son of Abraham. John the Baptist reminded the Pharisees that God could raise from the "Gentile stones" children unto Abraham.

Abraham's unwavering confidence in God was his most remarkable trait. Those who demonstrated the same spirit of faith would be justified even as he was and, therefore, included in the "family of the faithful" of which he was the father.

3:8—The scripture, foreseeing: It is, of course, understandable that Paul is not suggesting the Bible has an independent existence. This is a form of speech. It is the equivalent of saying that the Lord who inspired the Scripture made the statement. This certainly gives evidence of Paul's strong feeling that God controlled the content of the Scripture.

Would justify the heathen through faith: Paul's basic argument is carried forward. This significant statement about the heathen would be especially relevant to the Gentiles in Galatia. Abraham was taken from the heathen world and justified in the sight of God without circumcision or any of the other ceremonies which were given later. The fact that the Gentiles would have the full privileges of God's favor is clearly taught in many places in the Old Testament. The missionary message of the New Testament has its roots deep in the worldwide vision of enlightened Judaism.

Preached before the gospel unto Abraham: Some may find this statement offensive but it is a thoroughly reliable declaration. God formally and publicly announced the "good news" to Abraham that his redemptive love was for all nations. Of course, he did not know all of the historical facts concerning the birth, death, and resurrection of Jesus of Nazareth. His faith was not in these historical events but rather in the fact that God would make provision, in his own way, for the reconciling of the world unto himself. Abraham lived up to the light that he had in God's process of revelation. This was the "gospel" of his day. He believed it and received gladly God's will for his life at that time. Of course, we cannot be dogmatic about how much Abraham understood. Jesus said to the Jews, "Your father Abraham rejoiced to see my day: and he saw it and was glad" (John 8:56). The Jews regarded Abraham as a prophet. It is more likely, however, that Abraham saw the day of faith and recognized it as a day of clearer revelation rather than understanding all the historical events in connection with the incarnation. He rejoiced because he knew such a day was coming.

In thee shall all nations be blessed: The Hebrew permits "bless themselves" rather than "be blessed." This does not mean that the people could justify themselves upon the basis of their own deeds. Everything Paul has said up to this point refutes this contention. It would mean rather that when the Gentiles wished to pronounce a blessing on one of their own they might say, "May the God of Abraham bless you." This would be because they had accepted Abraham's God and knew of no higher invocation to use in expressing their good wishes and spiritual progress for a fellow Gentile. Paul was convinced history was not without purpose. It was God-planned to produce a glorious kingdom made up of all who would receive him by faith. Long before the law was given, God had provided for all people to be included in his plan and become beneficiaries of the prosperity and happiness which came from the overflow of Abraham's faith and belonged to all who were his spiritual heirs.

3:9—So then . . . blessed with faithful Abraham: Paul triumphantly pulls the strings together with a significant and logical conclusion. Those of faith are even then enjoying the full blessings of being a member of God's justified family. They are the ones who, like Abraham, "against hope believed in hope" and were rewarded with a unique standing before God. The Greek word for faith is clearly active rather than passive. They are "the believing ones" and have become, like Abraham, pioneers in the creative experiences of life.

3:10—As many as are of the works of the law: Those who insist on viewing their religious life from a legal state must understand the implication of this decision. If one sets up the requirements of the law as a standard for his salvation, he immediately becomes a miserable creature because he must face the fact he violates law continuously. The old cliché "no one is perfect" is descriptive of his spiritual state. Paul puts it stronger. According to him, those who do not do all that the law requires are cursed. This means they stand in a state of condemnation. The law, of course, had value. When properly understood, its function was essential. The law was given in order that man might be reminded not only of his obligation to live right in the sight of God but also of his complete inability to fulfil this obligation. As long as man understands this is the purpose of the law, the law is valuable to him. When, however, he attempts to evaulate how much of the law he has kept and concludes he has merit in God's sight because his record is good, then the law becomes a stumbling block to him and even a curse. The Judaizers were depending on the keeping of the law (this might also be called "good works") to bring salvation to them. Paul insists in his letter to the Romans (4:15; 5:16,18) that the law condemns and works wrath. It does indeed! The Holy Spirit of God uses the requirements of the law to bring conviction of sin to man.

3:11—No man is justified by the law: Those who reject the New Testament doctrine of "justification by faith in Christ" often refer to forensic justification as "legal fiction." They forget that there is another element in the experience of becoming a Christian other than justification. It is regeneration or the transformation of one's nature by the Holy Spirit. This comes because one has surrendered in faith to God in Jesus Christ not only as Savior but as Lord of life. All of this is made possible because of genuine repentance and the willingness to come to Christ with no claim of merit. On the other hand, when one seeks to be justified by performing good deeds, he does not surrender to one who can change his life by destroying the power of sin within him. There is no power within the law to subdue the sinful tendencies of man. In fact, quite the opposite! When one believes he has merited salvation because of his performance, he is in danger of burying himself even deeper in the hole of self-righteousness. When man is left to himself to work out his own righteousness, he is a miserable failure. Paul's continual emphasis is that it is utterly impossible for one to attain a right standing before God through his own personal efforts.

The just shall live by faith: Three times in the New Testament these words of Habakkuk 2:4 are quoted. In Romans 1:17 the emphasis is on "just" as Paul is emphasizing the man who has come to a right relationship with God. In Hebrews 10:38 the emphasis is upon "faith." In the Galatian letter the emphasis is upon "live." The Christian does not live in order to pile up merit in order that he may be justified before God. He lives through a faith relationship. Paul is not trying to prove his doctrine of justification by faith from this verse in Habakkuk. He is only illustrating it. He has already proved it from God's method of dealing with Abraham. He is rather amplifying a spiritual truth which is clear elsewhere in the Scriptures.

Some have misunderstood Paul's quotation from Habakkuk and felt that he did violence to the exegetical truth of the prophet's statement. There is only a slender difference in the Old Testament between faith and faithfulness and most Old Testament scholars believe Habakkuk's statement could be translated "The just shall live by his faithfulness." Accepting this translation should not be interpreted in any way as a compromise with the doctrine of "justification by faith" but rather to be intellectually honest at the level of Old Testament scholarship. The one who is justified by faith will be faithful in living. It is not the faithfulness that justifies him, but rather the consistency of life comes because of a fellowship with God which has its source in his faith in God for personal salvation from sin.

3:12—The law is not of faith: It is impossible to combine two things that are opposites. When one depends on keeping the law, he is leaning on himself. When he puts his faith in Christ, he is no longer depending on self but is trusting in Christ as his sole sufficiency. These two avenues by which men seek salvation are diametrically opposed. They are antagonistic to each other and simply do not mix. These two principles contradict each other. They are roads that have two different starting points and they, therefore, produce two different destinies. Findlay says, "From faith one marches, through God's righteousness, to blessings; from works, through self-righteousness, to the curse." In legalism the sinner *tries to make God believe in him*. In Christianity, the repentant sinner is content *to believe in God*.

The man that doeth them shall live in them: When one is caught in the vicious circle of slavery to the law as a means of salvation, he has no peace. He must give unwavering and perpetual obedience in order to obtain life. He finds himself in a vicious circle. Depression and eventually frustration become his way of life. There can be no peace. He must continue to perform; and failure in any phase of obedience means discouragement and defeat.

3:13—Christ hath redeemed us: Although the Greek word used here is not the usual one for a ransom transaction, it is nevertheless definite. This word is more general in its meaning. It signifies a purchase. It denotes buying up or purchasing anyone in order to redeem him or to set him free. Perhaps the reason Paul uses this word rather than the traditional *lutroō,* which is a more strictly technical word for ransom, is because Paul was not stressing the manner of redemption nearly as much as the fact of it. It certainly cannot be used in any way to minimize the metaphor of God's deliverance of the sinner from his guilt and enslavement.

Being made a curse for us: No one has ever suffered more scandalously than our Savior. He was pronounced a criminal by both the Jewish and the Gentile authorities. He suffered the hatred of men, but this was not his greatest pain. He was forsaken by God. The words of Paul are not too strong—he was made a curse for us. The prepositions in this verse and verse 10 are interesting. The great Greek scholar, A. T. Robertson, used to illustrate them by drawing a hanging sword suspended by a hair ready to drop at any moment. He called this "the sword of Damocles." He said, "This is the curse under which we are." He then wrote the preposition *hupo* below the point of the sword. This is the word translated "under." Paul said, "As many as are of the works of the law are under the curse." Robertson continued by referring to the Greek preposition *huper* which means "over" but is translated "for." He translated "Christ redeemed us from the curse of the law, having become a curse for us [over us]." Robertson, in his diagram, would write the word *huper* over the other word *hupo* but under the suspended sword. The third preposition was the suspended sword. The third preposition was the Greek word *ek* which means "out of." Robertson translated, "Christ hath redeemed us from [ek] the curse of the law." He would indicate this by an arrow labeled with the preposition *ek* showing that Christ, by coming in over us, between us and the curse, and by thus bearing our curse, has removed us from under the curse of the law. Robertson used to say, "There! You have the substitutional atonement. The word *huper* could mean nothing else than substitution under the circumstances."

Cursed is everyone that hangeth on a tree: This does not mean, of course, that one is cursed because he is hanged on the tree. It means rather that death by hanging was the outward sign of a man who was cursed. This was both the curse and the punishment.

3:14—That the blessing of Abraham might come . . . that we might receive the promise: Paul now returns to his basic contention from which he has departed. The promise to Abraham was fulfilled in Jesus Christ and his work. This was God's positive purpose from the beginning. Now that the curse has been borne and lifted off, the blessing can flow forth both to Jews and Gentiles alike. The law was the great barrier which separated the Gentiles and the Jews. Through the work of Christ it has been done away with and, therefore, the removal puts Gentiles on the same level with Jews. Both can receive the gift of the Holy Spirit. Compare the sequence of thought in Ephesians 2:14–18 and Galatians 4:5 with this verse.

3:15—Brethren: The use of the vocative relieves the tension that Paul felt might be developing among those who read his letter. Rather than continuing in a tone of reproach and reprimand, he sought to make his remarks cordial and winsome.

I speak after the manner of men: Although the works of God are far above men and, in the deepest sense, cannot be understood by them, many times these truths can be illustrated by an example in human life which parallels the situation. When a principle has been shown that operates at the human level, it can be applied to the spiritual problem. Jesus used this method also (Luke 11:13; 13:15; 14:5).

A man's covenant: The Greek word *(diathēkē)* may be translated "covenant" or "will." In English these are two different words. In Greek, however, the word can be used with both senses. This ambiguity can be maintained by translating "last will and testament." A problem arises, however, because a will cannot be valid until the death of the one making it. God's covenant or will required the death of the testator. The writer of Hebrews, however, handled the situation in a most dramatic and scholarly way (9:15–21). The contention in Hebrews is that the blood which was shed at the covenant sacrifice meant a death had taken place and, therefore, nothing can be added to the will—certainly not by the law which was given to Moses centuries later.

No man disannuleth or addeth thereto: Paul had been thoroughly liberated from the fetters of slavery to Jewish legalism. To him, the whole Mosaic system was a parenthesis, an interlude, in the march of God's revelation to his people. This one who had sought to fulfil the law so meticulously now insists with all his heart that it was God's promise to Abraham, not the law added, that was the true covenant of God with man.

3:16—The promises made: Paul now moves from a covenant in general to the specific covenant made by God to Abraham. He uses the word "promises" rather than "covenant" which seems more appropriate because the content had to do with promises of salvation.

And to seeds . . . And to thy seed: Paul makes much of the singular form of "seed" as opposed to the plural. It is his contention that the promises made to Abraham were not fulfilled in the multitude of his descendants but rather in the one descendant who was Jesus Christ our Savior. It is a strong argument and one which he uses convincingly. It is only fair to say that some scholars believe Paul was not at his best in this argument. They say the difference between the singular and the plural of the word is not as great as Paul implies from his argument.

Many technical scholars have commented at length on this and some have gone so far as to accuse Paul of using a trick of argument or a quibble which seemed more worthy of a "trifling Jewish Rabbi than of a grave reasoner or an inspired man." There is much which cannot be known about the words because we are ignorant of many of the finer intricacies' of the language. Some scholars have suggested that these words may have a force which we cannot now trace. Unless one is prejudiced against Paul and, indeed, against divine revelation, the meaning seems clear. As Lightfoot points out it is not a matter of grammatical accuracy but theological interpretation. Paul is not allegorizing. He is spiritualizing. Many Old Testament prophecies were fulfilled spiritually.

One of the proofs that a great genius was at work in revelation is that there are hidden so many truths in the Old Testament that come to light in the New. Often a statement of historical fact is true at one level in Old Testament days but is true at an even deeper level in New Testament days. This is as much a fulfilment of prophecy as the actual coming to pass of a historical prediction made hundreds of years before it happened. The intention of God's promise to Abraham was there would be a limitation in the fulfilment. Everyone would not be included as a recipient of the promises. It was Isaac, not Ishmael, and it was Jacob, not Esau, who received the promises. There was a limitation from age to age until the fulfilment of the promise which finally came in the Messiah, Jesus Christ. This verse paves the way for the next which will further amplify the truth that it is the promises of God to Abraham which show us the value of faith and its relation to salvation rather than the law which was given at a later period.

3:17—The law, which was four hundred and thirty years after, cannot disannul: Paul's chronology has been attacked, of course, by some who seemingly would discount his spiritual message by questioning his historical accuracy. Perhaps the best defense of Paul's reliability has been made by Alvah Hovey in *The American Commentary,* although Albert Barnes has defended Paul with equal capability. We cannot be certain at what point Paul begins the calculation. Actually, there are several different ways that he could be technically correct. On the other hand, he could have been speaking in round general numbers that were accepted in his day. We should always remember, however, Paul was not seeking here to give historical data but rather to remind the people that the law was given long after the promise and could not destroy or change it. This is Paul's purpose, and we should not get off into the wrong hypothesis concerning the accuracy of historical statements. This does not mean for one moment that we are saying Paul's statement is inaccurate. There is ample evidence to defend his integrity at this point. The law had an intermediary purpose, which we shall see later, but it did not disannul God's original covenant with Abraham. This promise was that in the seed of Abraham his promise would be fulfilled and this seed was Jesus Christ. It is on this basis that Paul adds to the force of his argument that man is saved by faith and faith alone—not the keeping of the law.

3:18—The inheritance: The promise made to Abraham was that he should be the heir of the world. This was fulfilled, of course, when the Gentiles became "Abraham's seed." In the second psalm God says to his Son, "Ask of me, and I shall give thee the heathen for thine inheritance, and the uttermost part of the earth for thy possession." In Jesus, Abraham received the inheritance of people from all nations as his spiritual descendants.

Be of the law, it is no more of promise: There cannot be two ways of obtaining this mediatorial way of salvation. Promise and law simply cannot be combined. It must be one or the other. There is a "once-for-allness" with reference to God's grace. When God has made a gift to one who is completely without merit, no later legal system imposed upon his descendants can alter this gift. The

Galatians must choose between God's way of being saved and that which man has invented. Paul realizes the utter impossibility of man entering heaven's gateway by his own efforts. To express it another way, a wandering sheep cannot find his way home to the fold. The Master must seek and find him.

3. Purpose of the Law (3:19–24)

3:19—Wherefore then serveth the law?: Paul has made his point clearly. He has been courageous in stating the problem and bold in answering it. He has insisted that the law was merely an addition to the mainstream of God's purpose not something fundamental in his plan. Paul then, as he usually did, anticipated the objection which some might bring concerning his position. He had proved his point but perhaps he had proved too much. Some would now be saying that he was leaving no place for the law at all. Paul realized that a Christian must recognize the rightful place of the law in God's eternal plan for the ages. Paul, therefore, must clear himself of the false charges of being called "antinomian" (against the law). He must show that God is consistent, and he must demonstrate the proper value of the law in God's work for man's salvation.

Added because of transgressions, till the seed should come: Paul did not mean that the law was to halt unbridled iniquity. He meant rather that people transgress only when there is a recognized standard of right and wrong. The law was provided in order to place the standard before men. It was to arouse conscience and make people realize they were falling short of God's standard for their life. Because of this, they deserved God's condemnation. When God's full revelation, however, came in Christ, the law was not needed to make men realize their shortcomings. The sinless Son of God caused men to see their personal impurity. The law might remain a useful discipline to show men their own inadequacy and the need for further revelation from God; but it could never be, after Christ came, that which brought a proper and fulfilling relationship between God and man.

Ordained by angels in the hand of a mediator: According to Jewish tradition, angels were present when the law was given. In the Septuagint Version of Deuteronomy 33:2 this truth is clearly set forth. Stephen's speech (Acts 7:38,53) seems to agree with this, and the author of Hebrews speaks of "the words spoken by angels" as being steadfast (2:2). Paul uses this Jewish belief as a way of minimizing the law. To the Jew, any true communication from God to man conveyed life. It was possible to live only by the word of the Lord (Deut. 8:3). Paul believed that, although the law came ultimately from God, it did not come directly from him. If it had been a direct communication, it would have brought life. The law did not convey God's living voice. It did not bring men into his presence. It only communicated his commands and regulations. God himself remained aloof from the people. The orthodox Jew would have insisted that the thunder and lightning in connection with the giving of the law revealed the glory of God's presence. Paul, however, contended that this indicated God was not present in person. To him, therefore, since the law was given by angels or through angels it lacked the glory of the life-giving power of a direct communication from God.

It is interesting that some scholars believe the Jewish stress on angels in connection with the giving of the law is the reason the gospel writers are careful to record all the visitation of angels in connection with the birth of Jesus. God was to come directly to man in the incarnation. There must be no chance that the coming of Christ was in any way inferior to the giving of the law. The law was given through the angels. Jesus came directly from God but all the events in connection with his birth were testified to and announced by angelic beings.

3:20—Not a mediator of one, but God is one: Some scholars say this difficult verse has had hundreds of interpretations. Any approach to its meaning should recognize the context. Paul has been arguing that the law which was given after the promise did not invalidate the promise. He was also insisting, however, that the law still had a purpose. This seemingly parenthetical statement between verses 19 and 21 goes back to Paul's original contention—the promise is superior to the law. It is actually more consistent with God's own character. The promise was given directly by God, but the law had been given through a mediator. This marks it as inferior to promise. The mediator of the law was not God himself. The law was given through Moses. It was given on the condition that the people obey it. The promise was different. It was given directly by God and all his sovereignty stood behind it.

It was not conditional. A human intermediary, acting between two parties, lacks the independent authority that God possessed when he made his promise to Abraham and through him to all believers. Hendricksen says, "He did this on his own sovereign account, directly, personally. He was speaking from the heart to the heart."

3:21—Is the law then against the promises: This is a similar thought to the question in verse 19. Paul makes one point but then he is quick to recognize that if this point is carried to extreme it can be a false and even dangerous teaching. The law is inferior to the promises but it is not an enemy of them. They have both issued from the same God though brought to man through different means. They certainly do not work in opposition to each other. Paul was as loyal as anyone to the basic principles of Judaism. He repudiates as emphatically as anyone a position that would eliminate law from the sphere of God's revelation. It was a necessary step in God's working out his purpose for the world through the Jewish people.

God forbid: The Greek words mean literally "may it not be so." This idiom is translated several different ways. It is one of the strongest expressions possible in the Greek language. We can feel in these words Paul's horror that anyone would imply a contradiction in the character of God. Moffatt translates this phrase "Never!"

If there had been a law . . . which could have given life: Paul intensifies his claim. If the law had possessed the power to quicken the spirit and produce life, it might have stood in competition to promise but this was not its function. It, therefore, had no power. The purpose of the law was to produce a consciousness of sin. It is this guilt before God that strips one of power in his life. Thus the law can never make a man spiritually alive. It cannot motivate him or place within him a born again spirit. At best, the law can only cause a man to see that there is no righteousness within him and make him realize he needs the righteousness of God in Christ which comes to those who, like Abraham, place their faith in the promise of God. The law is useful. It shows a man that which he needs but cannot, of himself, accomplish.

3:22—The Scripture: To us, the Scripture means both the Old and the New Testament. We Christians especially think of the New Testament when we hear the word. To the Jew and Christian

of Paul's day, however, the Scripture meant the Old Testament
—especially the first five books which were called the Law or
Torah.

Hath concluded all under sin: The law leaves no avenue of
escape to anyone. All are condemned equally. This does not mean
that every person has sinned as much as every other person. It
means rather that all have been grouped together as sinners and
imprisoned within the jail of condemnation. The Old Testament
has declared authoritatively that no one is free from the bondage
of sin. All are spiritual convicts unable to break their fetters.

**That the promise of faith . . . might be given to them that
believe:** The inclusion of all men in one sweeping decree lays the
foundation for redemption in Christ. The purpose of the law is not
to save. Its function is to reveal guilt. The source of salvation is
Christ. The promise flows out from God, and faith makes it possible for man to receive the gracious benefits of Christ's redemptive
work. Jesus gives what the law cannot give. He is the concrete
fulfilment of that which had originally been promised to Abraham.
Actually, this is not a new teaching. Grace and belief are opposed
to merit and works. Salvation never came through keeping the
law. In Christ and his redemptive work, however, we see the
full-fledged breaking through of God's redemptive activity.

3:23—Before faith came, we were kept under the law: It is
probably best to follow most interpreters and translate "before *the*
faith came" since the word is used here in a different sense. Hovey
speaks of it as "the system of doctrine of which faith is a distin-
guishing feature—the faith system." The book of Jude (v. 3) speaks
of "the faith which was delivered once for all to the saints." Faith,
of course, existed as a principle long before the fulness of the
revelation of God in Christ and to some extent is included in the
phrase "the Christian faith" which we use today. It is doubtful that
Paul actually would have seen a contradiction in the use of faith
in the two senses, but the emphasis seems to be here on that which
has been called the "system of salvation by faith in the Lord Jesus."

Shut up unto the faith which should afterwards be revealed:
There is present both the idea of confining and guarding. Alan
Cole suggests the phrase "in protective custody" to convey the
exact meaning. Man was without merit and unable to move toward his own justification. He must await God's grace; and this

grace, though partially revealed through the centuries of Old Testament history, was not brought to full light until Christ came and brought life and immortality to light in the gospel. This restraint was actually for the purpose of benevolent protection. When God fenced off his chosen nation from their pagan neighbors by various laws, he was doing it for their good, not merely to impose a grievous limitation upon their freedom. He was protecting them and leading them to become a peculiar people so they could become the channel of his blessings to the world. God worked with a wiser providence than they realized when he put his people in "protective custody" while they were awaiting the realization of the promise.

3:24—The law was our schoolmaster: The Greek word translated "schoolmaster" is one of the most interesting in the Greek language. It is literally "pedagogue" and signifies a tutor or a child-bearer. The one who occupied this office had care and control of the children. He was in charge of watching them, restraining them, and many times subjecting them to a rigid discipline. Some see in this word not the tutor but the slave who brought the child to the tutor. The analogy seems evident. By its pedagogical work, the law awoke a sense of sin in man and prepared him to receive with joy the redemption in Christ. This means the law could prepare people for fellowship with God through faith. This is a much higher status than merely perfunctory obedience to the mechanical requirements of the law.

Being justified by faith: The repressiveness of the law's discipline stripped from one any faith in human adequacy for salvation. There was thus no alternative to sinful man, falling short of God's standard, except to throw himself entirely in faith upon the One who is not only able but supremely willing to give the sinner a new standing before God and emancipate him from the bondage into which sin had led him.

4. Glorious Results of Faith (3:25 to 4:11)

3:25—After faith is come: Again, as in verse 23, the definite article accompanies the word for faith. This is the message of faith or the gospel rather than describing the individual faith of the believer (see further comments on v. 23).

No longer under a schoolmaster: The two principles, justification by faith and righteousness by law, cannot coexist. Once faith has entered the scene there is no room for law. Those who have come face to face with the teacher no longer need the pedagogue. They have a kind of freedom which they have never known. Servitude has passed away. They are no longer subject to their burdensome ceremonies of Jewish legalism. They are not haunted by guilt because of the condemnation which the law presents to them. They have seen their sin because of the law but they have seen something greater. They have witnessed the grace of God through the reconciling work of Christ into which they have entered through faith.

3:26—Children of God by faith in Christ Jesus: In Ephesians 2:3 Paul speaks of those in the pre-Christian state as "children of wrath." There is a great tendency among people today to call everyone indiscriminately "children of God." Paul's position is clear. The redeemed family of God is made up of those who have come through faith to the Father and been adopted into the divine household. This is one of the most assuring doctrines in the New Testament. When God comes into one's life and makes him an heir of the divine promises and a partaker of the divine nature, that person has all the rights and privileges implied in those terms. He no longer lives the immature life of slavery nor is he under a tutor. He is now a recipient of sonship because of his faith in Christ. Neither does he cease to become a son if he fails at certain points of obedience. If an earthly child disobeys temporarily and falls down the steps, he does not cease to be in the house of his father. Even if his body is bruised, he does not cease to be his father's child. So with the Christian life. We do not become a Christian by works. Neither do we retain our standing before God through good works. It is all of faith—a faith that is vital and meaningful and a faith that seeks to do good deeds for God's glory (but still faith)—that brings us into the new relationship of being a member of God's family.

3:27—Baptized into Christ—put on Christ: New Testament Christians associated the outward sign of baptism so closely with the inward change in the life of the believer that sometimes the two seem inseparable. It is unfortunate that through the centuries Christendom has debated so much concerning the necessity of baptism for personal salvation. The Scriptures clearly teach the symbolic nature of this act. The intimate relationship between Christ and the believer is set forth superlatively by the phrase "baptized into Christ." In Romans 6:4 the emphasis is upon the death, burial, and resurrection as symbolizing the death of Christ and also the death of the believer to his old life and resurrection to the new life. To the Galatians, Paul pictured baptism as putting on a garment which envelopes the person, and wearing it identifies his new life. An Old Testament figure of speech which is similar but not identical is where "the Spirit of the Lord clothed himself with Gideon" (Judg. 6:34). Baptism is meant to be a public act not a private one. It is a way of solemnly affirming one's entrance upon a new spiritual life of faith in Jesus Christ. It signifies a death to the old life and a complete commitment to all that Christ stands for and urges man to be and do. When one is baptized into Christ he becomes so thoroughly identified with him that he himself is not actually living but it is Christ who is living in him.

3:28—Ye are all one in Christ Jesus: In the divine family every barrier is swept away. There are no special privileges and there are no special disabilities. All of the conventional distinctions of society are eliminated. Lightfoot says, "One heart beats in all: one mind guides all: one life is lived by all. Ye are all *one man,* for ye are members of Christ. And as members of Christ ye are Abraham's seed, ye claim the inheritance by virtue of a promise, which no law can set aside." We should remember, however, that Paul did not mean that a Christian loses his individuality. Various facets of a diamond reflect beauty—each from its own angle. So each Christian should reflect the beauty of Christlikeness according to his own personality and in his own unique way. When we speak of "the unity of the faith," this does not mean a doctrine has crystallized until it has become static nor possessed of a deadly sameness. We mean rather that there is a unity and equality in the Christian faith in the midst of diversity. Each individual may retain his own function in the ongoing stream of life but all are related in a mystical union to the totality of believers who make up the kingdom of God—the body of Christ.

3:29—Abraham's seed . . . heirs according to the promise: When a person wished to become a member of the Jewish faith from another religion, there were three requirements. He must be cir-

cumcised, offer sacrifice, and be baptized. A candidate for Jewish
baptism must cut his hair and his nails and undress completely.
The baptismal bath contained enough water for every part of his
body to be touched by it. Three men attended him while he made
his confession of faith. Parts of the law were read to him while he
was still in the water and words of encouragement, followed by
benedictions, were spoken to him. When he came forth from his
baptism, he was a member of the Jewish faith. Paul, however,
knew how everyone, both Jew and Gentile, became a *true* child
of Abraham—in the spiritual sense. It was by receiving through
faith the promises made to that great patriarch. This is the spiritualizing of the promise. Paul was fond of interpreting the Old
Testament Scriptures in this fashion.

Does this mean that the promises to national Israel are canceled? This is a controversial point among Christians today. Many
say that there is a time in the future when Israel will be gathered
and dealt with by God once more in a unique way. Another school
of thought among Christians insists statements such as this one by
Paul mean there is no place in history for the Jew except as he
comes to Christ in faith. The cleavage is great. Christendom will
probably never be united on this point. One thing, however, is
certain. In this day Christians are spiritual Israel. They are recipi-
ents of the divine fellowship because they have received through
faith the revelation of God which was made in Jesus Christ. The
millenarians and nonmillenarians may continue their dialogues
and disagreements. The nontechnical student of God's Word finds
peace and joy in knowing he is a member of the divine family and
is, at present, enjoying fellowship with God because he, like
Abraham, has believed and it has been accounted unto him for
righteousness.

4:1—Now I say: Paul has proved his case well. He could have
ended his argument at this point. Once again, however, he anticipates the answer of his opponents. They would claim that he is
pouring contempt on those of the Jewish faith by making them
no better than slaves. Under the period of law, the promise lay
dormant. When it was revived, it was taken away from national
Israel and conferred on the heathen. Paul must answer this argument. He must leave no stone unturned in order to deliver the
Galatians from any possible error. We can feel the eagerness of

his soul as he ejaculates, "What I mean is this . . ."

The heir, as long as he is a child: In 3:29 Paul spoke of Christians as heirs. This provides the base from which he enlarges upon the concept in order to distinguish between the period before and after the coming of the promise. There is no inconsistency between the freedom of those who are now in Christ and the bondage in which they were held before their redeeming experience. One may be an heir and yet not possess the inheritance in all fulness. One who is still an infant is not legally qualified to exercise control over his estate. He is not yet ready to come into his rights. In such a state, he is actually in no better legal standing, at the moment, than a slave. He cannot control the property and is entirely under the control and direction of others. He must wait until he is of legal age to assume authority over the estate. The Greek word used for child means "babe" and literally designates "one not speaking." It is the same word used in 1 Corinthians 3:1 to signify one "who is still on milk" and "unable to face the solid food of Christian doctrine." In the Galatians context, however, the proper rendering is probably "a minor," for the emphasis of Paul is that the child is not old enough to inherit the property under the terms of his father's will.

4:2—Under tutors and governors: It is difficult to be absolutely certain as to Paul's meaning. The words "guardians and trustees" is a good translation. It is doubtful Paul meant any technical distinction between them and the schoolmaster or pedagogue of 3:25. The Lord could perform all of these functions without there being a contradiction in roles. Of course, Paul could have thought of the guardians and trustees as those who taught the law while the pedagogue was the content or the thing taught. If this be accepted, the "guardians and trustees" could represent the Judaizers and their activism in propagating the necessity of clinging to the law as well as accepting the redemption of Christ.

Up to the time appointed of the father: This expression should be seen as related to "the fulness of time" of verse 4. The one who bestows the estate has the privilege of fixing the time the heir shall have control of it. Some scholars have sought to disparage Paul's illustration by pointing out that in the Roman law of that day a minor whose father was dead was supervised by a guardian until he was fourteen and then by a trustee until he was twenty-five.

They argue that Paul's reference to "the time appointed of the father" is erroneous. The resourceful Ramsay, however, contends the passage reflects the old Seleucid law that allowed the father to appoint both guardian and trustee and set forth all of the requirements and privileges concerning the inheritance. Ramsay even uses this as a strong argument for his position that the people to whom Paul was writing were in *South* Galatia.

Moffatt doubts we have enough information for a firm decision and suggests that trusteeship and guardianship could well go on concurrently, being held by the same person or persons. According to him, the guardian might have a responsibility for the welfare of the minor and the trustee be in charge of the management of the estate. Even under Roman law it could well be true that the father could, at his will, set forth the time that he wished his heir to remain under trustees, with the government setting the time only if a person died intestate. Even though we may not know the exact legal situation, there is no doubt as to the religious teaching of the passage. The father may be dead or not dead and the heir still be potentially "lord of all" although not yet in possession of the estate.

4:3—In bondage under the elements of the world: The word translated "elements" means literally, according to Thayer, "any first thing, from which the others belonging to some series or composite whole take their rise." Thus it signifies an element or first principle. The word may be used of the letters of the alphabet, the material causes of the universe, the heavenly bodies, or the primary and fundamental principles of any science or discipline. When applied to religious thought, it indicates the crude and elementary ideas of religion which both the Jews and the heathens practiced in the early stages of religious development. There is debate among scholars as to whether "we" in this verse refers to pre-Christian Jews or whether it refers to the heathen as well. The Jews, of course, had a higher stage of religious revelation, and yet many feel that the burdensome ceremonies of Judaism were just as powerless and empty in God's sight as the superstitious forms of idolatry practiced by the heathen. Both held their devotees in slavery and represented a very elementary stage of spiritual development.

4:4—When the fulness of time was come: This phrase has been dealt with eloquently as related to many facets of preparation. It has been pointed out that the Greek language had spread through the civilized world and become virtually the universal tongue. The Roman roads facilitated transportation and communication. Jewish synagogues had been established in most major cities helping the Christian missionaries to reach Jews, Gentile proselytes, and God-fearers. These seem but superficial milestones along the road to God's preparation, however, and the spiritual evidences seem more significant. The educative work of the law had brought to man a sense of spiritual need because of guilt. Human nature had passed through every conceivable form of sin and iniquity. It was in deep need of the gospel's healing touch. Sin had caused the suffering world to pine deeply and cry in anguish for a word from God. In the divine wisdom the Savior came at the exact moment when, in God's judgment, it was best for the world to witness the fulness of revelation. God's purpose was, of course, predetermined in his wisdom and we shall never know why gloomy years were allowed to roll on while the world sank deeper in ignorance and sin. God works all things to his divine glory. Christ's coming was the turning point in human history and is properly called "the fulness of time."

God sent forth his Son: This is not a reference to Jesus leaving his home in Galilee to begin his preaching ministry. Paul is speaking of the incarnation. There is certainly implicit within this statement the divine drama of Christ's preexistence as well as his birth and life among men, culminating in his death and resurrection. It is interesting that the word used for "sent forth" is the one from which the term "apostle" comes, and Paul may have been making an allusion to the title over which there had been controversy with the Judaizers.

Made of a woman, made under the law: Those scholars who insist this first phrase cannot be taken as a reference to the virgin birth of Jesus are probably correct. On the other hand, Paul does seem to imply that Jesus had another nature than the one which was derived from the woman. This reference speaks of his full humanity which means he assumed all the limitations and weaknesses of mankind. If, however, he was merely a man, the "made of a woman" would appear a superfluous and unnecessary description of him. We must not, however, assume Paul knew nothing of the virgin birth. Luke was his constant companion, and it is inconceivable that Paul would have remained ignorant of information of such magnitude which was possessed by Luke and recorded in his Gospel record. Paul's expression would bring to mind two Old Testament passages. First, in Genesis 3:15 the writer spoke of the promised "seed of the woman" who would crush the serpent's head. Second, Isaiah had spoken of the coming birth of one who would be called Immanuel (7:14). The Savior was divine in the fullest sense, but he was also one who took upon himself human nature and was bound by all the requirements and subject to all the controls of a human being even though he possessed a unique relationship with the Father.

Made under the law: The definite article is not present in the Greek. Thus, Paul is not speaking exclusively of Jewish law. He would certainly contend vigorously that the Mosaic law was the highest and most rigorous form, but Paul would quickly extend the application to all of those who were subjected to any system of ordinances and regulations. Of course, the primary reference is to the Jewish race and legal system for Paul is dealing with this subject. His point is that Jesus humbly and willingly submitted to all of the requirements imposed upon those who were not yet ready to receive the promise and begin the life of redeemed sonship. He fulfilled all of the requirements of the law in order that he might be able to deliver from the bondage of law.

4:5—To redeem them that were under the law: Paul uses the same Greek word for redeem as in 3:13 (see comments there). Paul uses the same phrase "under law" as in 4:4 indicating that he had in mind humanity as a whole under the sway of both natural and moral law. In 3:13 Paul speaks of being redeemed from the "curse of the law" while here the expression is slightly different and seemingly a bit bolder. Paul speaks of being redeemed from law itself. It may be that Paul is speaking of law as a system of attempted self-justification and is stating that we are redeemed from our own efforts to bring ourselves into right relationship with God through good works. He certainly is teaching us that Christ was sent into the legal bondage and required to wear the legal yoke in order that he might shatter it to pieces with his atoning death.

That we might receive the adoption of sons: The first personal plural pronoun embraces all Christians—both Jews and Gentiles.

Some scholars believe the verb contains within it the idea of "getting back," but the general feeling is that "attain" comes nearer to expressing the thought. The phrase "adoption of sons" translates one Greek word. Although a legal term, it is used only in a religious sense in the New Testament. God not only delivers us from the awfulness of enslavement because of sin's evil, but he also honors us with the choicest blessing imaginable. In fact, it is practically impossible to find a human analogy for the concept of adoption. Those who receive it possess not only a new name and a new legal standing but have a new family relationship. In addition, the image of Christ is stamped upon them.

Paul has the order of the divine work in proper sequence. Justification must precede adoption. First, man's guilt is dealt with in the atonement as he is reconciled to God by the death of Christ. He is then made a member of the family of God as spiritual union takes place between the believer and the redeeming Savior. Paul expressed it in another letter, "When we were enemies, we were reconciled to God by the death of his Son, how much more, being reconciled we shall be saved by his life" (Rom. 5:10). We need to remember Paul's entire emphasis is that we have no claim of merit for this high honor. It is through grace that we become members of God's redeemed family.

4:6—God has sent forth the Spirit of his Son: To be a child of God means more than prestige and status. One must share the family life. This means one should be spiritually qualified to enter into full and free fellowship which comes because of the unique relationship with God. If one is united to Christ in a vital way, the presence of God's Spirit is an inevitable result. Paul sets forth the harmonious cooperation of all three persons of the Trinity in a beautiful manner. The same God who sent forth his Son at the proper time has now sent forth the Spirit of his Son. This exact phrase is not found any other place in the New Testament. In Romans 8:9, however, Paul speaks of "the Spirit of Christ" in a way that shows he does not make a distinction between the Spirit of Christ and the Spirit of God. Paul is dealing with a most important subject because it is the Spirit's presence within us that gives complete assurance that we are God's own and enables us to pray with confidence (Rom. 8:16).

Abba, Father: Jesus used this expression (Mark 14:36). The first word is Aramaic, which was the language of the Jews when they returned from Babylonian captivity. It was very similar to Hebrew and was spoken in the days of Jesus by many people, even by some far distant from Palestine. There is no doubt that Jesus spoke Aramaic some during his ministry. It is very probable that he used the expression often when he made reference to the Father. Because of this, it seems to have passed into the vocabulary of early Christians. When one is speaking in a language other than his native tongue, he will sometimes, in a moment of deep emotion, return to that native tongue for an expression of his innermost feelings. As Paul's heart responded to the Father's love, he, no doubt, felt that there was not a word in the Greek language which quite conveyed the meaning of the Aramaic word with which he was familiar. The presence of Christ's Spirit within his heart caused him to cry out in joyful recognition, overwhelming gratitude and filial trust.

A Jewish tradition says slaves were not entitled to use the expression "Abba" when addressing the head of the family to which they belonged. If this be true, Paul represents Christians as using the language of free people. There is a great lesson here—Christians have been freed from slavery—the bondage of sin.

4:7—Thou art no more a servant, but a son: The believer does not become a son because of the operation of the Spirit. It is rather that the presence of the Spirit in the heart is evidence of the believer's sonship. It is furthermore the basis of assurance for the child of God. The second person pronoun to which Paul changes makes the message more personal and impressive. It is as though he were speaking individually to every separate Christian in Galatia.

An heir of God through Christ: Literally, an heir through God. It seems more logical that Paul would have said "an heir *through* God," but he has been emphasizing sonship and has been thinking of God as the one by whom believers have been adopted. The thought uppermost in his mind was the privilege and glory of being made a child of God. Thus, he does not speak here of the channel through which this adoption can become a reality—the redemptive work of Christ. It is not that Paul does not hold Christ's death to be important in establishing the relationship. It is rather that he is thinking of the Father's great love to make such a relationship possible. This manner of expressing it climaxes the two phrases, "God sent forth his Son" (v. 4) and, "God hath sent forth the Spirit of his Son" (v. 6). It was God who bestowed the inheritance because of his great love and his unlimited resources. To be an heir of God means being "a joint heir with Christ" (Rom. 8:17) and promises a glorious destiny. Those who are redeemed children of God can find peace in waiting for their promised inheritance to become a reality. In the meanwhile, the Spirit of Christ is present in the heart now to give assurance that we are sons of God and not slaves to sin.

4:8—When ye knew not God: When one is in an unregenerate state, he cannot know God, in truth, because God can only be understood where he has revealed himself. Paul recognizes the partial excuse the Galatians had for their former condition. This does not mean they were justified but rather that he can understand why they were in bondage to inadequate and even "false" concepts of deity. It was when the true knowledge of God came to them that spiritual freedom emerged. Paul is not apologizing for their previous conduct when they were in bondage to false gods. He is merely emphasizing that higher understanding brings higher responsibilities. When light increases, judgment becomes stricter.

Them which by nature are no gods: This play on words is a familiar Jewish pattern of speech. The Hebrew language is unusually adaptable to this type of expression. Earlier, Paul spoke of the Galatians as being in bondage to the ABC's of the world—the rudiments or elements (see 4:3). Paul recognizes that the Galatians in their former state had assigned to these elementary things the value of God. Although Paul does not say it here, the worship of the state and of the spirit of Caesar could also be included in this category. In fact, all forms of heathen ritual, including that of demon worship, would be a part of this sweeping inclusive statement of Paul. It is difficult for us, in our enlightened state, to realize the tremendous darkness that was upon a people who had no clear concept of God because they had not received the full revelation. Yet, in our modern day, we are seeing on every hand society turning away from the full light of revelation and back to heathen concepts although they are presented in the framework of intellectual sophistication. This verse and the next are more relevant to our modern life than appears on the surface.

4:9—Have known God, or rather are known of God: Paul was anxious for the Galatians to avoid concluding from his first phrase that their relationship with God was because of their own ability or own adequacy. The essence of heathen worship was that by performing a ritual, accepting a creed, gazing at the stars, observing certain days, or involving oneself in mystic meditation you could climb the mountain of speculation and become in tune with the infinite. This is actually self-worship and an attempt to attain salvation by one's own merits. A constant temptation of us all is to attach undue importance to our recognition of God and minimize God's grace which has led us to Christ in spite of our sinful hearts and rebellious wills. The old phrase which has almost become a cliché "there but for the grace of God, go I" is still an excellent statement for us to bear in mind constantly and repeat to ourselves often.

The weak and beggarly elements . . . ye desire again to be in bondage: The redeemed man is still a human being and subject to all the limitations of the flesh. It is difficult, even for a regenerated person, to live in the spirit. He is constantly tempted to maintain a legalistic approach to morality and a superstitious dependence upon things which he should have outgrown when he surrendered in faith to the Savior. The continuing battle of the flesh *versus* the spirit can be won by the new man in Christ only as he grows into a real and spiritual fellowship with God. Lightfoot speaks of the worldly system as being "weak" because it has no power to rescue man from condemnation and "beggarly" because it brings no rich endowment of spiritual treasures.

4:10—Days, and months, and times, and years: It is difficult to be certain as to all Paul meant when he attacked the "rudiments" or elementary stages in religion. Most scholars follow Lightfoot's contention that although Paul recognized the complete superiority of Judaism to heathenism in the spiritual aspect, he saw a close affinity between the ritualistic aspects of the two. There seems no doubt, however, that these expressions refer to the liturgical calendar of Judaism although in a lesser way they could have certain veiled references to the heathen observances that were prevalent in Asia Minor.

4:11—I am afraid . . . lest I have bestowed . . . labor in vain:

Although Paul was preeminently a theologian, he was not inter-ested in establishing a theological system for its own sake. His concern was the salvation and spiritual growth of the people to whom he ministered. Neither was he anxious about his own fruit-lessness but rather for the people who stood in jeopardy because they either misunderstood or were not heeding the message of Christ. In some translations the word "somehow" or "perhaps" is present. If accepted as a legitimate rendering, it means that Paul has not definitely decided that his labors have been a waste of time. This may be called properly one of Paul's most pessimistic utterances in the entire letter, but we can understand it as a swinging of his emotional pendulum rather than a firm decision. It is certainly clear that Paul has not shut the door of hope on the people of Galatia. He is seeking to lead them to repentance and, though temporarily discouraged, he believes they will vindicate his best hopes for them.

5. Another Personal Appeal (4:12–20)

4:12—Brethren, I beseech you: It must have been disappointing for Paul to see people who should be free from laws and ceremo-nies exchanging their divine birthright for the childish toys of legalistic requirements. Thus far, he has presented an irrefutable case against the false gospel. He has explained and argued in order to destroy the web of sophistry which has entangled their minds. He now proposes another approach. He will speak with the per-suasion of love. The expression "brethren," which may be ren-dered "Christian brothers," is the strongest term of affection he has used thus far in the letter. Likewise, the word "beseech" is strong in emotional appeal. It not only means "ask, request," but in various places is translated "pray" and "supplicate."

One can feel the heartthrob of Paul as this tactful shepherd of souls follows his sharp reproof with a tender, urgent, and intensely personal appeal. It is as though he were pulling out all the stops in the organ of his soul and revealing his deepest self to them. He felt that the very essence of the Christian faith was at stake and the entire kingdom of God was at the crossroads. They *must* hear him. That is the passionate desire of his soul. He is not concerned about winning a victory over his opponents. He rather wishes to win his opponents to the freedom that is available in Christ.

Be as I am; for I am as ye are: Literally, the Greek says, "Be (imperative) as I because also I as you." The first phrase is easily translatable. The second is variously rendered. The tendency among some scholars today is to place the implied verb in the past tense rather than present. The RSV translates, "I also have become as you are" while the NEB translates, "Put yourselves in my place . . . for I will put myself in yours."

Paul is reminding them that, although he excelled in meticulous observance of the law, he had given up any thought of achieving justification in the sight of God by his good deeds. The Galatians had begun this way, and he is urging them to return to the point from which they started in receiving salvation through faith. Paul had relinquished all his special privileges as a Jew. He put himself on the same level as the Gentiles. He threw himself entirely on the grace of God and took his stand for Christ, not the observance of the law, as a way of salvation. Paul had no intention of forsaking that position. He is urging the Galatian Christians to do likewise.

This is a personal appeal for them to return to the fellowship with him that has been broken by the Judaizers, but it is even more. He is urging them to tear themselves loose from the legalistic position to which they have reverted and become as he—one who is trusting in simple faith in Christ for salvation.

Ye have not injured me at all: Paul has been called a "warm-hearted master-psychologist" and this phrase proves it superlatively. Paul anticipates the response of the Galatians. When they hear his appeal, they feel that if they come back to his position and receive him warmly, there will still be a gulf between them that can never be entirely mended. Paul protests strongly that he feels any personal injury because of their previous conduct. He is perhaps overstating the case a bit, but it is not a misrepresentation of the fact. Paul honestly feels that any injury done was more to the cause of Christ than to him personally. He is quite honest when he assures them they have not hurt him. He wants to make them completely comfortable and wishes them to have no anxiety concerning his future attitude toward them.

4:13—Through infirmity of the flesh I preached the gospel: There has been much speculation, and most of it without profit, concerning Paul's bodily weakness. At best, we can only surmise the nature of it. The text makes it clear there was some physical infirmity that paved the way for his preaching to the Galatians. Either he was detained there longer than he intended to remain or else he was led to go there contrary to his previous plans. What was this "bodily weakness" and how did it incapacitate him?

Some have suggested the stoning recorded in Acts 14 and some continuing effect of it. Again, it has been suggested Paul had a fever, perhaps related to malaria. The matter of Northern Galatia and Southern Galatia comes back into focus (see Introduction). It has been denied that the southern plateau was malarial or the section through which the missionaries had passed before coming there. Still others have suggested that the fresh breezes of the northern plateau would have been ideal for a sick man.

The book of Acts does not give us any help nor does it tell us of any time when sickness caused Paul to stay longer than intended at Galatia or any place. There is the suggestion, however, in several places that Paul was plagued by ill health. This may have been part of the reason Luke accompanied him—although not the entire reason.

From the eleventh chapter of 2 Corinthians we are led to conclude that the book of Acts is by no means an exhaustive account of Paul's sufferings but rather a greatly condensed and selective recording of significant incidents. Paul describes his problem as "a stake thrust into my body" (2 Cor. 12:7). This certainly suggests a painful and lingering malady. Many scholars, of course, insist Paul had difficulties with his eyes (see comments on 6:11) but this hardly seems relevant to the present passage.

It may be that in the search of scholars for a profound sickness they have overlooked the simple fact that Paul was a man who constantly pushed himself to the limit of endurance. His "weakness of the flesh" may simply have been an exhaustive condition which required a long recuperative period of rest. Perhaps it was not a nervous breakdown in the sense of our modern terminology but nevertheless Paul was, as we say, "completely run down" and had to rest for many weeks before continuing in his missionary journey. It may be that he was not too weak to do some limited preaching but had to "take it easy" and learn to "pace himself" before leaving the region of Galatia.

4:14—My temptation which was in my flesh ye despised not nor rejected: Literally, this reads, "And your temptation in my flesh you neither treated with contempt and scorn nor rejected (literally, spat out)." This unusual grammatical form causes RSV to translate "and though my condition was a trial to you, ye did not scorn or despise me" and NEB to render, "and you resisted any temptation to show scorn or disgust at the state of my poor body." Most scholars agree with this interpretation of what Paul is saying. The word which can be translated "spit" has caused some to see here a reference to epilepsy and has caused them to believe this was Paul's "thorn in the flesh." The evidence for this, however, is slender and this position is not generally accepted by scholars. Paul's point is clear.

It was difficult for the Galatians, as for anyone, to accept the spiritual authority of a man who was dependent upon them physically. This would be especially true when he was presenting a new and revolutionary message to a society that had little background for it and whose moral standards, especially among the Gentiles, were not in sympathy with the disciplines this new religion required.

Received me as an angel of God: This vivid contrast causes us to feel the eagerness and intensity with which the people welcomed Paul. In spite of his physical limitations, they treated him with the utmost respect and placed complete confidence both in him as a person and in the message he proclaimed.

Paul is speaking, of course, in harmony with their present knowledge of divine revelation. He is not implying that when he came there he found them in possession of a full knowledge of the gospel. He does not mean that they understood the doctrine of angels and associated him with one of the heavenly host. It is rather that the enthusiastic welcome they gave and the reverence they showed him was, as he looks back at it now, comparable to how a knowledgeable Christian would greet a heavenly messenger. There may have been, however, a slight allusion to Acts 14:-11–15 where we are told that the people at Lystra called Barnabas, Jupiter, and Paul, Mercurius.

4:15—Where is then the blessedness ye spake of: Although most scholars view this as an interrogative statement, there are some who believe it should be interpreted as a rhetorical question. The words "ye spake of" are not in the original text. They are interpretative and should have been printed in italics. If this is to be regarded as a rhetorical question, it has the force of an exclamation.

What overflowing joy you possessed! How happy you were with tender affection! What blessings and favors you poured out on me! But this joy has gone. The interrogative force would say, "Why are you not still enjoying the ecstasy that was present when you first received Christ? Was your rejoicing shallow and, therefore, meaningless or were you sincere in those days and have merely allowed your relapse into legalism to rob you of the joy you could be experiencing even now? You were congratulating yourselves but now you are suffering deep feelings of guilt because you have left the simple and yet blessed teaching of the gospel for enslavement in the shackles of a legalistic system.

Plucked out your own eyes . . . given them to me: There are many scholars who see here a reference to Paul's "weakness in the flesh" and contend he had some kind of ophthalmic disorder. They see further reference to this in Galatians 6:11 (see comments on this verse).

Scholars are divided on this question but Lightfoot has strong conviction against it. He maintains the emphasis of the Greek is not on "your eyes" but rather on your "eyes." This means, he contends, that the thought is not that the Galatians were to put out their own eyes for him but rather that they would have gone to any extremity to help him even to the giving of that which might be considered their most priceless possession. He sees a relationship to this expression and that of the psalmist, "Keep me as the apple of thine eye" (Ps. 17:8).

4:16—Become your enemy because I tell you the truth: This sentence is introduced rather abruptly. This is probably because of the emotional state in which Paul was at the time of writing. The word "enemy" should not be considered in the passive sense "hated by" but rather in the active, meaning "hostile to." This means Paul was asking the Galatians, "Do you think I am hostile to you because I am telling you the truth?" rather than saying, "Have I become hated by you because I tell you the truth." Again, this can be considered a rhetorical question expressing exclamation rather than interrogation.

Paul is, of course, not expressing the matter as he looked at it but rather inquiring the view which the Galatians were disposed to take toward him. Paul knew he was not hostile to them but he feared they had become quite enraged at him because he was insisting on maintaining the purity of the gospel even at the expense of losing their affection.

4:17—Zealously affect you, but not well: The verb means literally "have strong affection toward." It is very closely connected with the verb which means "to seek." The Judaizers are courting the Galatians. They are displaying great affection toward them but their motivation is not honorable.

Would exclude you, that ye might affect them: The verb translated "affect" is the same as in the previous phrase and has the same basic meaning except the situation is reversed. Paul does not specifically state that from which the Judaizers wished to exclude the Galatians. There are two distinct possibilities and perhaps both are included in Paul's statement.

First, the Judaizers would shut out the Galatians from Christianity itself by insisting those who followed Paul's gospel were not genuine followers of Christ. Connected with that would be that the Judaizers were attempting to drive a wedge between the Galatians and Paul. What would be the result? In either or both cases they would turn to the Judaizers for correct instruction. Paul makes no attempt to conceal his feeling toward the Judaizers. They have ulterior motives. They wish to gain a following for themselves. By claiming to be the only true Christians they "excommunicate" all who disagree with them.

4:18—The literal reading of this verse is abrupt and might be even characterized as a "fragmentary mode of expression" rather than a smooth polished sentence. Paul often resorted to this type of expression when he was emotionally involved in a situation.

Although the exact translation may be disputed because the language is highly compressed, scholars are generally agreed as to Paul's meaning. He recognizes the value of loyalty to one's leaders, whoever they are. He realizes he cannot have a full monopoly on the people at Galatia and that when he is absent others must minister to them. He does, however, resent the Galatians not having sufficient depth and insight to recognize leaders who are exploiting them for personal vanity rather than ministering to them in an unselfish way.

The word "affected" should be translated exactly the same way as in verse 17. There is no "play on words" intended. Paul is submitting a thinly veiled reproach to the Galatians because of their fickleness. When he was with them, they sought after his advice diligently and followed him implicitly. While he recognizes he must share their love and loyalty with others, at the same time, he does resent their growing so cold toward him and actually rebellious at the message he taught. Zeal is good, Paul would say, but it should be tempered with judgment and respect for the one who introduced them to Christ in the first place.

4:19—My little children: There are two Greek words *teknon* and *teknion* which are very similar. The first means simply "a child," that is a descendant or one's posterity. The latter means a "little child" and is used as an endearing term. In John 13:33 the plural is translated "my dear children." It is the general opinion of scholarship (although a few differ) that the correct textual reading should be "my little children." This represents a breakthrough for Paul.

He has previously called the Galatians "brethren" (4:12), but now he uses this term of intimacy which expresses the closeness of the bond that exists between them. This relationship between a minister and those whom he leads to personal faith in Christ is a unique and exclusive one. Paul never denied the importance of Christian growth but there was a unique relationship between him and those who were his personal converts to Christ. They were his "joy and crown" (Phil. 4:1). He felt he had a special claim on them which superseded these new teachers.

Travail in birth again until Christ be formed in you: This figure of speech shows the yearning love and painful agony which Paul felt for these weak and misguided converts. Love surges into every part of his being as deep anguish takes hold of his soul. This deep solicitude and painful anxiety is comparable to a mother in birth pangs. Paul had this experience once in their behalf. He feels again this great agony. This time, however, it is not for their experience of regeneration. Paul realized one could not be born spiritually the second time any more than he could be born physically the second time. It is for their growth that he is now concerned. He wishes them to become mature Christians in every area of their understanding and living. There is a great lesson for both evangelists and pastors here.

It is good to have a zeal for converts, but it is also pleasing to God if we have a similar zeal for their growth and development. The expression "Christ . . . formed in you" speaks of a quality of life which is much needed today. The adjective "Christlike" best expresses the thought. One becomes Christlike when Christ is formed within him. It means Jesus Christ indwells the believer and becomes the ideal for all this thoughts and deeds.

4:20—Desire to be present with you now: A chord is struck in Paul's memory when he thinks of his earlier experiences with them. It vibrates for a moment and he gives expression to his feelings. He was conscious of the time and space limitation. Because of his busy schedule (regardless of where he was when he wrote this letter, Paul remained a busy man), he could not drop everything and rush to Galatia. He realized his converts had lost much by his absence. Because they had changed their views, they had to some extent become alienated from him. He felt he could restore the personal relationship if he could correct them concerning the teaching. Although a letter should be helpful, he felt he could accomplish much more by his personal presence.

Change my voice: There have been two suggested interpretations of this phrase. First, the apostle regretted his severe language on his second visit to the churches. He wished to modify his tone and speak with gentleness. If he could see them in person he could talk in a more tender and affectionate manner even though he still spoke the truth without compromise. Another suggestion has been that the expression "to change my voice" meant to change to some other means of expression. This means Paul was contrasting a personal visit to them with the sending of a message through the written word. A. T. Robertson says, "Paul could put his heart into his voice. The pen stands between them. He knew the power of his voice on their hearts." The two meanings are not, of course, mutually exclusive. In fact they supplement each other. For a parallel instance when Paul regretted harsh words that he used, see 2 Corinthians 7:8.

I stand in doubt of you: Paul was at his "wit's end" concerning the fickle Galatians. His writing contains a mingling of speaking with authority and at the same time pleading through love. He was both grieved and baffled. He spoke with anxiety and yet with rebuke. He was puzzled as to how he might find an entrance into their hearts. This particular Greek word was found in the Papyri of the second century in describing a man who was "ruined by creditors and at his wit's end." Paul was concerned about the solidity of their Christian principles and felt frustrated because he did not know the solution for their dilemma. His love, however, had not failed. He continued to be long-suffering and kind and patiently hope for their deliverance from their blindness and bondage.

6. Illustrations of Freedom in the Gospel (4:21–31)

4:21—Tell me, ye that desire to be under the law: Paul has used every type of argument and appeal that he knows about, but a fresh idea occurs to him. The Jews were steeped in the rabbinical style of argument. He decides to use this type of reasoning in order to meet his opponents on their own terms and in their own style. The expression "law" means probably not only the Pentateuch, but the complete body of revealed truth—the Torah. Of course, Paul's illustration is from the Pentateuch but it actually precedes the giving of the Sinaitic legislation. Lightfoot points out that the definite article is missing in this phrase whereas in the next phrase it is present. (See comments on 4:4–5).

Do ye not hear the law: Paul's tone is both lively and penetrating. Rather than demanding their respect he is now commanding it. Paul was perfectly at home when it came to discussing the Scriptures. No one could surpass or even equal him. If it is law they wish, he only asks that they follow the law to its entire and logical conclusion.

4:22—For it is written: This phrase introduces a general reference to Old Testament history and might better be translated "it is stated in the Scriptures." It does not introduce a direct quotation for a proof text but rather an historical happening that will serve as the basis for a spiritual lesson.

Abraham had two sons: Since Paul's opponents and those Galatians who followed them in their teachings prided themselves on being physical descendants of Abraham, Paul wishes to remind them that there were two biological offsprings of Abraham. If mere physical descent from the patriarch is so important, the Ishmaelites have as valid claim as the Jews for God's favor. Paul is now ready to discuss the controversial question, "Who are the true heirs of Abraham?" Paul knows he can show the Judaizers that the descendants of the child who came by promise are the true sons of Abraham. The historical account concerning the birth of these two children may be found in Genesis 16 and 21.

Bondmaid . . . freewoman: The entire controversy has already been rehearsed and acted out in Abraham's family life many years before. The bondmaid is used exclusively in the New Testament for a servant. The word is also translated handmaid. Paul does not moralize concerning the wisdom of monogamy and the dangers of polygamy, but since we live in the full revelation of God we can easily see the poisonous feuds which have resulted because of this unwise relationship between Abraham and Hagar. It is interesting that Paul seems to take for granted that his readers would be familiar with the history of Abraham and his children. This indicates either a large majority of the Christians were from Jewish background or else that they had been thoroughly oriented in the Old Testament Scriptures.

4:23—Born after the flesh . . . by promise: Ishmael was the fruit of the natural biological process of procreation. Isaac's birth, on the other hand, was because of the grace of God. He had promised to give Abraham and Sarah an heir. She was far past the age of childbirth, but God blessed her with a child. Isaac was Abraham's child by the flesh but he was more than that—he was a child of promise. There was a distinct difference between the two children. Both had the same father, but their conceptions took place with radically different attitudes toward God's promises.

Ishmael has been called "the fruit of unbelief" because Abraham became impatient with God and his promise to give him an heir. Ishmael was the son of a slave and in an inferior position from his birth. His was a state of servitude and he remained in this capacity throughout his whole life. He thus represents those who base their hope for salvation on what they are able to do—their own works.

Some scholars see a double sense to Paul's use of "born after the flesh." Ishmael was born as a result of carnal deliberation—the physical desires of Abraham and Hagar as well as the impatience of Abraham for an heir. This may be getting more out of the text than is there, but we are certainly safe in seeing here a picture of all who labor slavishly to attain their own salvation rather than trusting Christ and knowing the joy of a faith relationship with God.

Isaac was "spirit born." This does not mean he was conceived by the Holy Spirit as was our Savior, but it was God's Spirit who caused the promise to be fulfilled. It is not improper exegesis to say that Isaac is a symbol of all people today who are "born of the Spirit" in a regenerative experience.

4:24—Which things are an allegory: Generally speaking, scholars are not impressed with allegory as a means of teaching truth. Men such as Philo and later Origen abused this method of interpreting the Scriptures and caused it to fall into much disfavor. On the other hand, Paul is using the method on a high level. He does not deny the literal truth as allegorists might do nor does he even minimize it as most allegorists did. To Paul, an allegory was a spiritual truth which was embodied in history. Moffatt speaks of "a shadow from the eternal world cast upon the sands of time."

Paul felt God's divine principle could be present in a historical situation even though it was demonstrated on a larger scale later in God's plan of the ages. He would have insisted that since God is changeless his spiritual truths are also changeless. When we conceive of allegory in this fashion, it becomes helpful but we must always keep our allegories within the disciplines of reasonableness and consistent with other revealed truth. As William Hersey Davis used to say vehemently, "Allegory is not proof." G. G. Findlay insists, however, that Paul's allegory and that of the general allegorical school of his day were different—as "widely removed as the 'words of truth and soberness' from the intoxications of mystical idealism."

The two covenants: The basis of allegorical interpretation was that words, figures of speech, and even grammatical form had a spiritual significance in addition to their literal meaning. Paul is now applying the basic thesis of his book to the story of Sarah and Hagar. He has insisted that the covenant of promise was the true covenant and the basis of it was faith. The covenant symbolized by Hagar was the one which was not of faith but rested on performance in order to bring about God's promise rather than the simple trusting of God to do his work. If one refused to have faith, he forfeited his claim to be a true child of Abraham. The two sons were not literally the two covenants but rather represented the two covenants—one on Mount Sinai and the other which is made with the people of God in the gospel but was foreshadowed by the one made with Abraham.

4:25—Agar is Mount Sinai in Arabia: Some scholars have gone to great lengths and much ingenuity to find a reference to some specific mountain in Arabia. This, however, is unnecessary. It is entirely unrelated to the rest of the analogy. Perhaps one reason earlier commentators were so anxious to find a "local reference" was their belief that Paul spent three years in the region round about Sinai (see 1:17). Many modern scholars today, however, feel this reference to "Arabia" means the area in the immediate vicinity of Damascus which, at that time, was under the control of the Arabian leader, Aretas. We cannot be certain as to Paul's knowledge of the southern desert where Sinai was located. On the other hand, we also cannot be sure he did not visit there.

Answereth to Jerusalem which now is: The expression "answereth to" can be translated "marches with." It is used of soldiers as they dressed ranks. It may be used of any ideas which are in similar categories. When Paul compared the existing Jerusalem with the covenant of bondage, it must have frustrated and even infuriated the Judaizers.

If one follows the entire logic of Paul's argument, he was actually saying that the present Judaizers were children of Ishmael in the spiritual sense rather than children of Abraham because they were depending on works for their salvation. This was certainly a most unwelcome form in which Paul put his argument but unless he had exposed them in such a radical manner he could not have shown the true position of the legalists. The Judaizer was actually no better off than the person living in Judaism. He was loaded with self-inflicted legal requirements. In spite of their professed keeping of the law, the Judaizers were slaves to sin and in servitude to their pride. They lacked the nobleness and the elevated faith of their fathers. Although they vaunted their liberty, they were actually servants of sin and bondage. Their religion had no justice, mercy, or faith. They were punctual in the observance of the external requirements of the law but their nature was completely unchanged. Their hearts had never been touched by the warm glow of faith and love.

Regardless of their robes of outward decorum, they were naked in God's sight. They were the personification of law without grace. They claimed to be free, but they carried the soul of a slave. The Jerusalem which existed was not the city of promise but the city of slavery. When one bases his hope for salvation on his own good deeds, he is engaged in an empty and futile work.

4:26—Jerusalem which is above: The present Jerusalem was full of injustice and was subject to the tyrannical rule of the Roman Empire. In contradistinction, however, to this Jerusalem of slavery there was an ideal city. It was not seen at present, but in God's plan it was destined to supersede it.

What was this "Jerusalem above" of which Paul spoke? It already existed in Paul's day in heaven because Christ was there and the souls of those who died in Christ were present with him. It is also, of course, the city "that will be" in the consummation of the age. It is also true, however, that this city exists on earth now—in a mystical sense. God's true kingdom—his heavenly city—consists of all born-again believers whether on earth or in heaven.

This Jerusalem above is the believer's true habitation. Since he is a citizen of the heavenly Zion, he breathes the air of divine freedom. Some scholars have pointed out that Paul mixes his metaphors slightly but this is no real problem. He draws a contrast first between the present Jerusalem and the future Jerusalem. He also then draws a contrast between Jerusalem below and Jerusalem above. There is no real inconsistency. It is the heavenly Jerusalem which is "the mother of us all" and the whole concept of "New Jerusalem" is an eschatological one. Yet, the whole approach is realistic and rooted in history because living believers constitute a spiritual kingdom now. The Orthodox Jew loved Jerusalem. The Christian Jew loved the geographical Jerusalem also but he, even more, loved the true city of God.

4:27—This verse is a quotation from Isaiah 54:1 and in the original context was a direct reference to Israel who had been made desolate because of the exile in Babylon but was now being told to rejoice because she was being delivered from captivity. In the prophetic passage the woman who is without a husband and barren is the Jerusalem of exilic days while its inhabitants were in captivity. The woman with a husband is pre-Exilic Jerusalem. Whether or not the prophet had Sarah and Hagar in mind in his original utterance we cannot be sure, but Paul saw this as a marvelous illustration of the point he was making concerning Abraham's two wives and descendants. The chief thought is, of course, that the New Jerusalem, representing those who seek salvation through faith, will far surpass in glory the present Jerusalem which is a symbol of those who seek their justification by works of the law.

Paul was seeking by every possible argument to shatter every defense of the Judaizers. In this passage he was meeting the counter-propaganda of those who insisted that only a radical fringe of foreign Jews agreed with Paul's interpretation concerning freedom from the law of Moses. If one claimed Paul's followers were upstarts and consisted of those rejected by the orthodox group and scorned because of its small membership, Paul answered that there was a time when Jerusalem was despised by her opponents. He even used Hagar as an example of the non-Jewish world who would eventually be blessed through the grace of God.

It must have been shocking for the Judaizers to see Gentile Christians already exceeding in number the Jewish Christians. It would have shocked them even more had they realized that the time would come when Gentile Christians would even outnumber non-Christian Jews. This prophecy would eventually be fulfilled in a far deeper sense than any of that day could realize. We accept these truths with little or no surprise. To people of that day, they were revolutionary thoughts.

4:28—As Isaac was . . . the children of promise: There is a sense, of course, in which Ishmael was also a child of promise. The angel of the Lord said to Hagar, "I will multiply thy seed exceedingly, that it shall not be numbered for multitude" (Gen. 16:10). The promise made concerning Ishmael, however, was made after his conception. God's promise concerning Isaac was made to Abraham and Sarah while Sarah was still barren and it seemed virtually impossible that she could conceive. Lightfoot speaks of the course of nature being suspended in the conception of Isaac. Paul, in this verse, once more calls the Galatian Christians "brethren" which indeed they were as Abraham's legitimate sons and true heirs because of their faith.

All true believers are members of the same family. There was nothing "natural" about the new birth. It thus corresponded to the birth of Isaac which, although not supernatural in the same sense as that of Jesus, was, nevertheless, contrary to the ordinary laws of nature.

4:29—Persecuted him that was born after the Spirit: Once more Paul resorts to the traditional exegesis of the rabbinical school. The allusion is to Genesis 21:8–9 where we are told that on the day Isaac was weaned Abraham made a great feast. Sarah saw Ishmael mocking. The original lacks the words "her son Isaac" but this is added by both the Septuagint and the Vulgate and, beyond doubt, was what the writer of the Hebrew text had in mind. Ishmael was fourteen years older than Isaac. He was thus about seventeen at this time.

There is some doubt as to the correct translation of the verb which the King James Version renders "mocking." Some scholars believe it means merely "playing with." The interpretation would then be that when Sarah saw the two boys having a good time together she was afraid they might become joint heirs of Abraham's wealth and this was offensive to her. Because of this, she demanded that Ishmael be sent away. Other scholars, however, insist this verb does not refer merely to innocent fun. The same verb is used in Genesis 19:14 concerning the "jesting" which the prospective sons-in-law of Lot did as they greeted the announcement of Sodom's coming doom. The verb meant "coarse ridicule" or "mockery." For other examples of this Hebrew word see Genesis 39:14, Exodus 32:6, and Judges 16:25. None of these refer to simple innocent fun.

The most likely meaning is that Ishmael was probably showing the same attitude toward Isaac in play that Hagar had shown toward Sarah—that of looking with contempt upon him (see Gen. 16:14; 21:9). This is the basis for Paul using the expression "persecuted" to describe the way that non-Christians were treating those who were followers of Christ. This was true, of course, in a special way concerning the attitude of the Judaizers toward the born-again Christians.

Those who are not Christians, whether immoral people or overbearing legalists, are offended when they see Christian people happy in the Lord. The wicked world will cast stones in any way possible in an effort to destroy the joy of a believer in Christ.

4:30—What saith the Scripture?: In controversial matters Paul always insisted the final verdict should be arrived at by examining the written Word of God. He was certain that the record of God's revelation to man in history contained the authoritative verdict and the one which would meet the deepest need of the human soul.

Cast out the bondwoman and her son: This is a quotation from Genesis 21:10 which is actually a statement by Sarah to Abraham. Paul accepts it as an authoritative statement from which he secures allegorical truth. He would justify his treatment by contending that any word of Scripture whose validity is demonstrated by experience may serve as a basis for allegorical interpretation. This was a guideline among those who practiced exegesis of this nature. On the other hand, however, it is significant that in verse 12 God confirmed her demand and instructed Abraham to obey Sarah's injunction. He adds the explanation that it is through Isaac Abraham shall find ultimate fulfilment of the promise made to him. Some manuscripts and later translations add the words, "for she is a prophetess."

Shall not be heir: The slave boy had no proper birthright and therefore no proper footing in the house. He represented a constant threat to the boy who was the true heir. He exceeded his limited privileges and made himself intolerable. It was necessary that he be cast out of the home. Paul's teaching is clear. It is those who trust Christ for salvation who are accepted by God. Those who rely upon performing legalistic requirements for divine favor are rejected. Law must give way to the gospel. Judaism must be separated from Christianity. Those who continue to maintain with fanatical zeal that the keeping of law is necessary to salvation are spiritual Ishmaelites not Israelites. They must either be converted or removed. In the language of today they must "shape up" or "ship out." There can be no compromise.

4:31—So then, brethren: This phrase represents a conclusion to the entire section (vv. 21–30) rather than merely a further amplification of verse 30. Paul is not saying we should be followers of Isaac because Ishmael suffered such a terrible fate. There was always, of course, an element of warning, whether expressed or not, in Paul's exhortations to give one's allegiance to Christ. There was a much broader base, however, for the conclusion in verse 31. The entire contrast between Abraham's two sons and their mothers with all of the allegorical interpretations and implications pointed to the conclusion in this verse which summarizes the section.

Not children of the bondwoman, but of the free: The literal Greek says, "Not children of *a* bondwoman but of *the* free." The absence of the article gives a qualitative emphasis while the presence of the definite article makes the expression refer to a specific person, Sarah, and allegorically to the Christian community. Paul's statement thus means that there is a great gulf between one seed and the other. Those who belong to the group represented by the seed of the bondwoman want to inherit the promise of God some other way than by faith in Christ. This disparages the redemptive work of God and glories only in the accomplishments of self. On the other hand, those who have identified with God through faith in his son have a new spirit dwelling within them. The deepest potential of a man is thus fulfilled in the Christian gospel.

We are made to be free and we attain the highest and best in life when we are free. As we saw earlier (4:9), Paul considers bondage to the ordinances of Judaism as virtually analogous with the superstitions and fears of heathenism. On the other hand, freedom from the law, and the dread of its curse, plants within man the ability to overcome the frustration because of human weakness. He can face life with creativity and find fulfilment in a dynamic fellowship with Christ.

III. Moral and Ethical Obligations
5:1 to 6:10

Paul's first two arguments for his position were from history (chaps. 1–2) and from doctrine or scriptural exegesis (chaps. 3–4). He has one concluding contention which is convincing and powerful. It is the moral argument—his appeal to the great transformation which has come because of the freedom in Christ.

The Jewish law, with all of its prohibitions, could not produce such a change in life. It is only personality that can transform personality and the dynamic presence of Christ in the life of the believer does that which no set of rules could ever accomplish.

This final section hammers home the moral and ethical obligations of the gospel message. Paul is anxious that no one consider him as a preacher of antinomianism. Liberty in Christ does not mean license to do anything one's lower nature wishes. If this were true, the Judaizers would be justified in their condemnation of Paul's gospel. Paul recognized the importance of the issue and dealt with it effectively in this last section. One is not wrong in considering these two final chapters the glorious climax to the letter.

There are two schools of thought concerning 5:1–12. Some scholars consider it to be the final part of the section which begins with 3:1. This would make it the conclusion of the doctrinal emphasis of the book. Other scholars, however, consider 5:1 as the beginning of the practical section in which Paul calls upon the Galatians to put into everyday living the moral and ethical implications of the theological content. Paul's usual pattern in his letters was to lay a broad base of doctrinal teaching and then call for practical application in everyday living.

There is actually no way to settle the question as to which main division these verses should be assigned. It is perhaps proper to consider them as a transition between the two, emphasizing freedom in Christ but reminding the Galatians of the doctrinal framework into which that freedom fits along with the ethical obligations which it brings to the life of the redeemed person.

Beginning with 5:13 the ethical emphasis definitely begins. Liberty does not mean license. When one is motivated by Christ, the problem of fulfilling the law fades into the background. The flesh and the Spirit are in constant battle. Each produces its own results. Paul lists them in 5:19-23.

The final part of the section deals further with the attitudes and actions of the man who lives in the Spirit. He is to be kind in his relationships to others, humble as he considers his own weaknesses, generous to those who share with him in Christian teaching, aware of God's moral and spiritual laws, and patient in waiting for vindication.

1.   An Earnest Appeal to Proper Use of Freedom (5:1-12)

5:1—Stand fast therefore in the liberty: Many scholars consider this verse as the conclusion of the previous section rather than the beginning of a new one. Some modern versions print this verse as a little paragraph all by itself. It is obvious that Paul changes from an argumentative style to exhortation and persuasion. He has certainly made his case concerning the freedom of a Christian. We must remember he based this freedom on the fact of redemption. Apart from the atoning work of Christ there is no true freedom.

Much that passes for freedom today in the political world is actually anarchy. So the same in our spiritual life. Some people misunderstand the difference between freedom and license. There is, however, the other danger—freedom must not relapse into slavery. Grace comes through Christ and freedom is the ripened fruit of grace. Freedom is disciplined by one's personal experience with Christ and by his love for spiritual things.

One must stand fast in Christian convictions, but he also must be unwavering in refusing to adopt legalistic restrictions concerning matters of policy and conduct. The Christian life is one of joy because there are basic principles, not rules, by which one's life is guided. All of this, let it be said again, is undergirded and overshadowed by one's personal experience with Christ in forgiveness of sin.

Entangled again with the yoke of bondage: Natural man is so

wrapped up in the idea it is his righteous deeds which bring justification in the sight of God that it is difficult to get this notion out
of his mind. Paul uses the metaphor of oxen hitched to a yoke to
picture those who are seeking to be justified by deeds of the law.
These animals toil all day long. They graze along the dusty road.
When they can no longer muster the strength to draw the burden,
they are slaughtered. Likewise, those who are seeking to be saved
by good works are slaves. They become discouraged, tired, and
broken down as they are constantly seeking to obey a set of laws
or perform a needless ritual. Paul is not dealing with an unimportant matter. To be liberated from the bondage of sin and God's
wrath is not merely a passing occurrence. It is rather a fulfilling
experience and a permanent joy. The yoke of the law is likewise
perpetual slavery rather than temporary inconvenience.

Martin Luther says, "Rightly are the doers of the law called
devil's martyrs. They take more pains to earn hell than the martyrs
of Christ to obtain heaven. Theirs is a double misfortune. First
they torture themselves on earth with self-inflicted penances and
finally when they die they gain the reward of eternal damnation."
If this seems putting it strongly, we should remember that Luther
lived in an unusual period of history. There is, however, the same
emphasis in many places today on being "saved by one's own
works" and such a doctrine is just as enslaving to one now as in
the days of Luther or Paul.

5:2—If ye be circumcised, Christ shall profit you nothing: The
situation in Galatia was an unusual one and, therefore, the acceptance of circumcision had a special meaning. It was more than
yielding to a custom—it was the acceptance of a principle and the
commitment to a legalistic relationship to God based on conformity to statutes. This left no place for faith and the development
of a spiritual life through the presence of Christ in the heart and
fellowship with him in a growth experience. Paul did not consider
for one moment any form of syncretism in concepts of religion.
To him, Christ must be accepted by faith, and the entire Christian
life must be a growing experience in fellowship with him or else
Jesus Christ could be nothing.

Behold, I Paul say unto you: Paul thought that if anyone was
qualified to speak authoritatively concerning the relation of circumcision to one's religious life it was he. Having been formerly

a strenuous contender for the utter necessity of observing the Mosaic law and having been converted through a life-changing experience, he is now in a position to speak solemnly and authoritatively concerning the matter. It is clear that Paul expected his authority to have considerable weight with the Galatians.

5:3—A debtor to the whole law: Paul's reasoning is if the Galatians consider circumcision as necessary to salvation they are contending the death of Christ was not sufficient. They are actually not trusting his death and resurrection to save them. They are trusting a system of works. Consistency requires they follow this school of thought to its logical conclusion. To do so would mean they are obligated to obey every technical requirement of the Jewish legal system. To Paul, circumcision was the seal of the law. If one willingly underwent this rite, he was entering into a contract to fulfil all of the law's requirements. He could not find his justification in the grace of Christ. He has entered into another way—that of trusting his own good deeds for righteousness in God's sight.

Once a person takes a certain road he is obligated to go all the way down that road. The only solution is to turn around and come back to the starting point and take another road. Salvation is either all of grace or none of grace. It cannot be part of each.

5:4—Christ is become of no effect unto you: This phrase is difficult to translate satisfactorily. The literal Greek has only three words. There is a verb (in the passive voice) and the words "from Christ." This verb has been variously translated. Perhaps the idea in Luke 13:7, where the same verb is used, is most applicable here. The Galatians have become useless or unproductive in their present state. Christ is not their inspirer because as long as they seek to be justified by their good deeds they cannot know the dynamic of a Christ-motivated life.

Ye are fallen from grace: There are two spheres of life in which men may live. In writing to the church at Rome, Paul expressed it as "the law of life in Christ Jesus" and "the law of sin and death." To the Galatians, Paul conceived of the two ways of life as "justification by grace through faith" and "attempting to be justified by the law."

Those who find their vindication by grace through faith in Christ are those who live in the spirit and do not have confidence in their good works. This is the highest level upon which one can live. When one is trusting anything other than Jesus Christ for salvation, he has automatically excluded grace as a means of salvation. One concept excludes the other. One cannot reconcile the "bookkeeping god of legalism" with the gracious God who receives men because of their faith. One cannot live as a slave to that which legalism calls for and at the same time trust in God's all-sufficient grace. Paul recognized the incompatibility of the two principles and expressed it with finality.

This verse should not be used to show that one can be "saved today and lost tomorrow" if he does not "hold out faithful." Paul is not discussing here the matter of "once saved always saved" but is showing the utter folly of trying to combine two religious concepts which are mutually exclusive and actually antagonistic to each other. One must live either in the realm where grace is operative or renounce completely faith in Christ as a means of personal salvation.

5:5—We through the Spirit: Lightfoot wisely observes that it is sometimes impossible to determine whether "spirit" refers directly to the Holy Spirit or not. He points out, however, that one actually overlaps the other because that which is spiritual within a man, if it is rightly guided, will be a reflection of the indwelling of God's divine Spirit. The emphasis of this verse falls upon the first part of it rather than the second part which probably has an eschatalogical inference. The contrast is between the flesh and the spirit even though the word "flesh" does not occur.

Circumcision was a thing of the flesh but justification before God has nothing to do with the "natural" part of man. It is entirely the work of God's Holy Spirit. Paul probably uses the plural pronoun "we" in order to identify himself with the Galatians even though they were not as solidly established in the faith as he and were showing signs of accepting a legalistic approach to Christianity which was diametrically opposed to his gospel.

Wait for the hope of righteousness: Of course, anyone who is familiar with Paul's teachings knows that to him the believer has already received a "verdict of acquittal" and his guilt is removed because of his trust in the atoning work of Christ. In this sense, his righteousness is an accomplished fact. He is not required to "hope for it" as something he may attain in the future if he performs enough good deeds. Although God has smiled his way into our hearts with justification, there is a day coming when we will be vindicated in the sight of men. It is this "blessed hope" of which Paul is speaking and which may be designated as the "hoped for righteousness." Believers are living under grace and are waiting with complete confidence for the fulfilment of the hope that they shall stand before him and be acknowledged by him at the final day.

By faith: All of the Christian life is lived in a vital relationship of dependence upon Christ and trust in him. It is true that we "have been" saved, "are being" saved, and "shall be" saved. There is no contradiction in accepting all of these statements as true. Man is justified by faith, he lives by faith, and with faith he looks for the consummation of all things. The one whose life is bound up with the observance of laws and ceremonies in an effort to secure justification before God knows nothing of the joyful experience of union with Christ through loving fellowship. There is absolutely no room in the Christian life for the spiritual life of faith and the slavery produced by depending on legal observances in order to obligate God in our behalf. Faith must be everything to the Christian, or it will be nothing.

5:6—Neither circumcision availeth anything, nor uncircumcision: Although Paul rejected completely the value of circumcision in securing favor before God, he just as quickly contended that uncircumcision, of itself, is also without value. He acted just as promptly to forbid the Gentile to boast of his uncircumcised state as he did to prevent the Jew from boasting of circumcision as the sign of religious superiority. Because of Christ, either position on the question is entirely irrelevant. Man is not justified because of his circumcision or unjustified because of his lack of circumcision. The Christian faith has one design—it wishes to abolish rites and ceremonies in order that it may present to the believer a salvation applicable to everyone on the same terms.

Faith which worketh by love: The constant teaching of the New Testament is that faith has great power. When it operates through the channel of love it is able to lay hold of both God and man. Inwardly, the life of a Christian consists of faith toward God. Outwardly, the Christian life is reflected in good deeds. This verse shows that Paul and James were not "poles apart" in their teaching but rather supplemented each other. Faith is the root of the new life in Christ. It is not merely an open hand wishing to receive but is rather a hand anxious to serve because it is motivated by an energetic working principle. Faith waits for his righteousness to triumph, but while it is waiting, it is working courageously in a spirit of love. Faith is adventure. This explains the service of men such as Luther, Wesley, and Grenfell but it is an adventure that cannot become reality unless love is the prime moving force. A life is transformed by faith but it is a faith which issues forth in both a loving attitude and loving service.

5:7—Ye did run well: This verb is a metaphor from the athletic world of the Greeks. Actually, no conscientious Jew could have had a part in the Greek contests because the men ran entirely unclothed and the contest was also related in a routine way to the worship of the heathen gods. Nevertheless, Paul felt he could use the metaphor as an illustration without placing his moral approval on the activity.

Who did hinder you that ye should not obey the truth: The progress of the Galatians had been arrested, but the apostle remembered with quickened feeling the zeal of the Galatians when they were pursuing the true Christian way before the deplorable hindrance arose and corrupted their thinking. The apostle now has finished his controversy with the Galatian Christians. He has made his case strong and has sufficiently chastened and corrected them. He is now ready to discharge a few remaining arrows in his quiver, but they will be directed more to the ones who are troubling the Galatians than the believers themselves.

The question in verse 7 is not asked for the purpose of information. It is rather a rhetorical question and expresses Paul's utter inability to understand why the Galatians would be led astray by people who did not have their best interests at heart. Ridderbos says, "The question is not prompted by ignorance, but by amazement. What kind of people were these false teachers anyhow and what did the Galatians expect of them, to warrant such an about-face?"

5:8—Cometh not of him that calleth you: The Galatians, in following the Judaizers, are actually saying no to no one but God himself. This is a mild way of assigning to the Judaizers the place of Satan. The distortion of the only true gospel is rooted in the one who would destroy them completely. The Galatians must never think their listening to the Judaizers is related in any way to a divine message. These foes of Paul's gospel are putting pressure upon the Galatians, and it is a pressure which is in diametric opposition to all that Jesus Christ taught and, if accepted, would invalidate and make without meaning his death on the cross.

5:9—A little . . . leaveneth the whole lump: This same expression is used in 1 Corinthians 5:6 with reference to the immoral conduct and influence of the man guilty of incest. According to Paul, if this is allowed to continue, the entire moral life in the Corinthian church will be corrupted. Scholars believe this expression represented a current proverbial saying.

The basic meaning is, of course, that there is always the tendency in any influence, even though it is seemingly small, to spread until it dominates an entire situation. The particular application of this principle to the local situation at Galatia raises a question. Was it the false teachers or was it the erroneous teaching to which Paul alluded?

There may have been existing among the Galatians from the very beginning a slight tendency to observe the customs and conform to the rites and this had now pervaded all of the people like leaven. On the other hand, it could be that Paul compared the false teachers to leaven. Although their doctrines were few in number, they had circulated throughout the entire Christendom of Galatia. Even more, it can be that Paul had in mind that any conformity to the Jewish legal system was like leaven. The people may begin with circumcision but they would not stop there. The legalistic approach would spread until all the doctrines of their religious life would be infected and they would come to observe every ceremony demanded by Jewish law.

It does not seem necessary to choose any one of these meanings thus excluding the others. Error comes in at first as a small and seemingly unimportant thing and not worthy of any particular attention or alarm. Later, however, when the doctrine has been completely infused into the Christian community one finds it has spread like leaven until the whole mass has become contaminated with the malignant error.

5:10—I have confidence in you through the Lord: Paul was a master strategist in dealing with people. When it was necessary to rebuke them, he was equal to the occasion. But he never despaired of the possibilities of those in whose heart Christ lived. When we look at things from a purely human standpoint, we are inclined to pessimism but Paul refused to view life in this way. He turned with abruptness from the discouraging aspects which seemed to be overshadowing the situation and expressed his hopeful confidence. In the literal Greek, the first person pronoun is used separately rather than being included in the verb. This emphasizes his strong personal confidence in the Galatians. It is as though he were saying, "Whatever others think about you, I believe in you with all my heart."

He that troubleth you shall bear his judgment, whosoever he be: If we had only the first phrase "he that troubleth" we might consider it as referring to a particular individual, whether identified or not, and this action could be considered as either present, past, or future. The rest of the phrase, however, has caused scholars generally to believe Paul is not referring to a particular individual, which he has identified mentally, but rather is speaking of anyone who in the future may disturb them.

Perhaps Paul's language is purposely veiled and somewhat indefinite. This would fit into the apostle's plan of putting the Galatians on guard so that if any creator of confusion approaches they may identify him with Paul's admonition and warning. Paul does not enlarge on the kind of punishment the troubler will experience. There is no reason for us to believe that he is referring especially or exclusively to the eschatalogical judgment spoken of in Romans 2:16. He may include that, but Paul certainly had in mind that his gospel would be vindicated on earth in the sight of people rather than merely at the end of time.

5:11—If I yet preach circumcision: Before reading any further, one should turn to the commentary material on 3:5 and give it careful consideration. The real problem of 5:11 is what foundation could there be to bring such an accusation against Paul? He was denying that circumcision was necessary for the Gentiles and yet some were accusing him of preaching circumcision. Was this because some remembered that he advocated circumcision before his conversion experience and were calling him one who yet (still) was preaching circumcision? Was it because for a short period after his conversion experience his position was a narrow Jewish one in which he insisted on the necessity for circumcision? Neither one of these contentions is strong enough to be seriously considered.

In all probability, those who claimed he was a "preacher of circumcision" did not understand (or did not want to understand) Paul's true position concerning the relationship of Judaism to Christianity. Everything that was good in Judaism could and should be retained by a Jew when he became a Christian. It was only when these things were considered as necessary for salvation or contributing to salvation that they became wrong.

Paul did not wish for the Jewish-Christians to give unnecessary offense to the non-Christian Jews. When no principle was involved, Paul could be very flexible. If, however, there was a spiritual issue at stake, he was uncompromising.

Paul believed in Christ's all-sufficiency for salvation. He could, however, accept circumcision for a Jew because it was a part of the Old Testament discipline that included some marvelous moral teachings. Any ritual that was connected with salvation must be ceased. The sacrificial system which pointed toward the atonement was no longer in effect because Christ had died for the sin of the world. Teachings concerning purity of life were just as binding as ever before and Paul was quite agreeable that circumcision should be included as one of those Old Testament requirements which a Jew might, and probably should, continue practicing.

There is a great law of psychology here. When we want to believe in someone, we will seek to understand his position. If we have "written him off" and decided we have no confidence in him, we do not even try to understand what he is saying with reference to a matter. The Judaizers had become determined in their efforts to discredit Paul and they grabbed at every straw for a chance to downgrade him. To insist that he was a preacher of circumcision was utterly false and any fair-minded member of the Galatian Christian community would recognize this fact immediately.

Why do I yet suffer persecution: The enemies of Paul cannot have it both ways. Either he is preaching circumcision or he is not. Paul could probably partially understand why they would persecute him for preaching against the necessity for circumcision for salvation. He realized it was cutting across their basic contention.

But Paul could not understand why they would accuse him of preaching circumcision and at the same time persecute him for his strong firm stand against the necessity for circumcision for salvation. The hopeless inconsistency of the Judaizers was far greater than their charge of inconsistency on his part.

Then is the offense of the cross ceased: The crux of the charge against Paul was his doctrine of the sufficiency of Christ's death on the cross. The unbelieving Jews saw in the cross a stumbling block. They used the Greek word *skandalon* (scandal) to describe their feeling concerning it. The non-Christian Jews simply could not believe a messianic pretender who had been executed for treason was, in reality, the Son of God who had been raised from the dead.

Far less could they believe that in the death of this one was that which atoned for man's sins. This was contrary to their concept of the coming Messiah and was utterly offensive to both their aesthetic beliefs and their religious convictions. Paul could have perhaps compromised with the Judaizers who were not so strong in their opposition to Jesus of Nazareth. He could perhaps have found a "middle ground" with them by insisting on faith in Christ as Savior but agreeing that circumcision and the law were necessary in addition to faith in Christ. But Paul insisted that the cross was the wisdom of God and the power of God and that Christ alone was necessary for salvation.

In this verse Paul's argument runs as follows, "You say I am preaching circumcision. If I were preaching circumcision, I would be eliminating the offense that comes because I insist that the cross alone is sufficient for salvation. If I eliminated this offense, I would eliminate the grounds of persecution. But I am suffering persecution. This proves I am still insisting that Christ alone is sufficient for salvation. It seems clear then that since I am still suffering persecution I have not eliminated the offense of the cross by preaching circumcision." As Hendriksen says, "Therefore, the all-sufficiency of Christ crucified for salvation, completely obliterating the need of any additional props such as circumcision, was the stumbling block for the Jews. But if the apostle were still preaching circumcision as a means of salvation, that offense would have been removed. Also, in that case Paul would no longer be persecuted by his kinsmen. Hence, the very fact that this persecution had not been discontinued was adequate proof that the charge of the opponents was false."

5:12—I would they were even cut off: The shock of this statement does not appear at first reading. The surface meaning of the King James translation is that Paul is suggesting those who are unsettling the Galatians should be excommunicated from the Christian community. The meaning, however, is much more drastic.

The New English Bible translates this verse, "As for these agitators, they had better go the whole way and make eunuchs of themselves!" What did Paul have in mind? He was, no doubt, thinking of the priests of Cybele who castrated themselves believing they were acquiring great merit in the sight of their god by such severe and drastic action. Paul's reasoning would be that if physical cutting could bring salvation these pagan observers were actually bringing greater assurance to themselves than those who observed the Jewish custom of circumcision.

Paul's language was, of course, blunt and shocking. Many delicate people would have been offended even as we might be if somebody made fun of Christian baptism by suggesting that if we are that "water happy" we should go on and drown the candidate and do a good job of it! Several things, however, should be taken into consideration before we condemn Paul too severely.

First, Jesus spoke quite severely when he said, "But whoso shall offend one of these little ones which believe in me, it were better for him that a millstone were hanged about his neck, and that he were drowned in the depth of the sea" (Matt. 18:6).

Also, we should remember that these were important days to the development of Christianity. The Judaizers were undermining the purity of the gospel and Paul felt deeply concerning the necessity for an undiluted witness.

Again, we should remember that Paul was writing under a unique inspiration and is responsible to God and not to us. After all, God alone is the one who has the ability to judge the moral and ethical value of Paul's statement.

A final observation might suggest that rather than criticizing Paul we might turn the spotlight of examination upon ourselves. We, too, are living in a day when the distinction between saved and unsaved is rapidly disappearing. In our effort to be tolerant to all people we stand in great danger of losing the ability to "glow with righteous indignation" when the truth of the gospel is compromised.

Of course, Paul was speaking with sarcasm and irony! His limit of endurance had been reached and he was anxious for one final statement that the Galatians would never forget. No one can deny he scored! He is now ready to move on to the section that emphasizes the spirit-filled life with its moral and ethical obligations. He has expressed his burning contempt for the Judaizers. His language was strong but no stronger than the conviction of his heart!

2.   Liberty Is Not License but Love in Action (5:13–15)

5:13—Ye have been called unto liberty: This is no new thought for Paul. He has already declared it emphatically, but this is a transitional sentence. In a sense it points backward. The "for" with which the verse begins suggests the reason for the statement, but the greater significance is that it comes now to introduce a completely new aspect of the subject. Paul has been contending that those who have found liberty in Christ should not fall back into the bondage of legalism. In the following verses, however, his emphasis will be that they should realize the full implications of their newfound freedom.

Use not liberty for an occasion to the flesh: There are two extremes which Christianity must constantly avoid. They are present in contemporary society and they likewise existed in Paul's day. One is legalism and the other is unrestrained indulgence which is a perversion of liberty.

Christianity has been likened to a bridge over these two polluted streams. One must not lose his balance and tumble into either side. On the one hand there is the narrow, bigoted, self-righteous attitude of those who believe virtue comes from adopting a pattern of conduct based upon the doing or not doing of certain things. On the other hand, there are those who fall into the gross vices of paganism and when they are corrected by anyone fling up the banner of "liberty" or "personal freedom" as though they dwelt in a rarefied air of sophistication far above the common man. The fights for liberty have been the supreme struggles of history.

When one achieves freedom, however, he has not arrived but

has only come to the beginning of a long journey. Moral and spiritual passion must be mastered if freedom is to endure and be meaningful. Unbridled liberty is a great enemy rather than a dear friend. Many dark sins have crept into life under this beautiful banner. There are two sides to the coin of being a Christian. We have the privileges of sonship, but we also have the ethical duties which are implicit within this new relationship. There is a great danger when untrained nature has liberty conferred upon it. The situation is similar to that of a nation that has won its freedom through conquering external foes but has an even more difficult battle. It must prevail over its own inner self.

Christianity has, in all generations, been called upon to defend itself against the charge of fostering lawlessness. The gospel has had to bear the reproach of those who have insisted that security encourages sensuality. A true interpreter of Christ will make it abundantly clear that a "finished salvation" does not mean the absence of moral and ethical demand. When truly understood, it means an even more stringent self-discipline but one based upon and worked at from within the context of a loving relationship with God through faith in Christ.

By love serve one another: There can be neither fear nor slavery when love is present. Even duty becomes a pleasant privilege when life is governed by the law of love. The truly free person is the one who is completely in bondage to the principal of unselfish love. The dearer the relationship, the stronger the bonds! Faith causes the authority to move from the realm of the flesh to the realm of the spirit; and love both conquers and unites.

Love does not need a bribe or a threat. It labors and waits in order to minister to those in need. It will brave a thousand dangers, will keep the hands busy and the eye watchful. It desires to render service gladly and willingly. Unless freedom is motivated by love it is empty and meaningless. It can never ease a broken heart or bring joy to one in distress. A ship without love, even though it possesses complete independence, will drift without a rudder and have no haven or horizon. We have become sons of God in order that we may be free, but the only freedom is to be enslaved by love. When we do a thing because we must, the hard coercion becomes a bitter experience. On the other hand, when we are motivated by love, the most painful service can be gladness and joy. This love level should be our constant goal.

5:14—All the law is fulfilled in one word: Although Paul protested vehemently against binding believers to the law in an arbitrary sense, he, nevertheless, recognized it as an expression of God's will. These words of Paul are strikingly paradoxical. He has sought thus far to dissuade the Galatians from slavery to the law. Now, he speaks to them of "fulfilling the law." We should remember that the word "law" is used in different senses. Legalistically, it may refer to the statutes of the Pentateuch but dynamically divine law was an ethical principle.

Statutes are important and should not be glibly ignored, but long before Paul wrote to the Galatians the statutory law itself had given the basis of its own fulfilment (Lev. 19:18). This truth becomes even more significant when we realize that Leviticus is preeminently the book of priestly legislation. Occupied chiefly with ceremonial and civil requirements, it, nevertheless, contains within the midst of the legal minutiae the sublimest and simplest rule of the Christian life. Certainly, Jesus did not come to "destroy the law" but to fill it full of its own self.

Shall love thy neighbor as thy self: Paul does not say that this attitude is a "summing up" of all the laws into one comprehensive statement. He is rather speaking of realizing the full maturity of the law. The legalistic requirements are both completed and consummated in the love of Christ and the adoption of his attitude toward the needs, both physical and spiritual, of both lost and redeemed humanity. The things which the law could never do, because of its multiplicity of requirements and redoubled threats, unselfish love manifested in positive and concrete action has accomplished at one stroke when Christ gave himself for our redemption.

The moralist contends that duty is the supreme virtue, but duty waits for its dynamic and finds it only in unselfish love. Law and duty may outline the path, but only love can give the will and power to follow it. One must not overlook that which is being emphasized by alert scholars today. We are not told to love our neighbor "instead" of ourselves but rather "as" ourselves. This implies that one must have respect for his own person if he is to show a proper attitude toward others. It is the one who has found liberty in Christ and is assured of his sonship because of the Lord's redemptive work who possesses the proper evaluation of his own selfhood that is essential to render service to others.

5:15—Bite and devour one another: The Greek word used for bite was used often in connection with animals but more frequently it signified "abuse." The other verb has the idea of "gulp down"; and since it is employed in such close connection with the former, we get the idea Paul was alluding to the conduct of the Galatians as more nearly representative of wild animals than Christian brethren. The Greek tense suggests that Paul is speaking of that which is in existence at the present. The people were in great strife because of the divisions in the church as a result of the false teachers. Paul is concerned lest the people in their spiritual warfare drive each other to a condition that would make it virtually impossible for them to be restored to proper fellowship in the Lord's work.

Take heed that ye be not consumed: If the Galatians continue to act as animals rather than loving Christians, there will be mutual destruction. Although Paul phrased his statement as though it were a hypothetical case, there seems no doubt he believed the conditions actually existed. He was, no doubt, not dealing with a few petty and personal rivalries but with a controversy that had already become deep-seated. It was more than an academic disagreement. The tides of passion and vindictiveness had already flowed freely, and Paul was concerned lest it gain in intensity and destructive power. The verb translated "consumed" conveyed the idea that nothing remained. This verb is used often of the devastation wrought by fire.

Paul was convinced that the surest way to annihilate the influence of Christ in Galatia was for the spirit of contention to continue. The fellowship would be destroyed and the happiness of the members be turned into frustration and emptiness.

3. Spirit and Flesh in Constant Warfare (5:16–18)

5:16—Walk in the Spirit . . . not fulfil the lusts of the flesh: Because the Christian life is often pictured as a journey, the word "walk" may be considered equivalent to "live." Paul was convinced that there was more than the lack of alliance between flesh and spirit. There was a deadly feud. It is impossible for a Christian to serve one if he is giving his loyalty to the other. When these antagonistic forces are at work within the heart of a believer, he must give his full allegiance to the rule of the Spirit or else he will be destroyed by the opposing power.

Paul believed that the law and the flesh were closely related and moved within the same sphere—that of outward and material things. If one has renounced the flesh, he must also renounce the law as a means of justification. In the original Greek there are no articles before "Spirit" and "flesh" which seems to suggest "two irreconcilable ways of living in sharpest contrast." The word for lust (translated "desires" in RSV) signifies the whole inner drive, that upon which man expends all his energies. Paul means more than the physical body when he speaks of flesh. He is referring to all the tendencies, impulses, and the inclinations of man's lower nature.

This verse, in all of its implications, describes the totality of man's life—both his relationship with God and his treatment of his fellowman. It is a promise that one who has left the realm of the flesh and come into the sphere of the Spirit will be victorious over the temptations that would pull him downward and destroy his happiness.

5:17—These are contrary the one to the other: In the life of a believer there is constant warfare. When one gives up the external authority of rules and guidelines, there is a natural impulse for his physical desires to run riot. The internal presence of the living Christ, however, brings moral power. It is the Spirit which safeguards man from bondage to the flesh. It is not correct to consider "flesh" as synonymous with the physical body. It is rather the raw, physical stuff of human life. Some people almost literally worship their physical drives. The flesh itself is not sinful, but when it is put in command of life it becomes the harsh tyrant that enslaves an individual. Of course, an opposite attitude is not the answer to the problem. It is unrealistic to consider everything physical as unclean. The real issue is the matter of who is in control of one's life. God has made the physical as well as the spiritual part of man, but when one is giving way completely to the lusts of the flesh he is in revolt against God's highest purposes for him.

Even a regenerated man has tendencies to evil. The matter of his personal growth in spiritual things will determine his tendencies toward things of the flesh and things of the Spirit. As the indwelling Christ becomes more of a reality in his life, the Holy Spirit will give him the victory over those things that are of the flesh and are harmful to him. The Christian is not to give way to the command of the flesh because this enslaves him more deeply but is to surrender to the control of the Spirit which will assure his freedom.

5:18—Led of the Spirit . . . not under the law: In the early stages of their Christian experience the Galatians had followed Paul's teaching and lived in dependence upon the Holy Spirit. The divine nature had been implanted and the power of the sinful nature had been broken. The Holy Spirit had taken up permanent residence within them. But when the Judaizers came, the Galatians became confused. They were still endeavoring to live Christian lives but they were using the wrong approach. The element of self-dependence had come into focus and caused them to inject their own good works by observing the law as a substitute for dependence upon a Spirit-led life.

Paul recognized, of course, the danger that could come to an immature Christian when the restraining influences of law were removed. A libertinism could develop which would be just as bad, if not worse, than a life of hypocritical self-righteousness. The path he suggested was not a middle road between the two. He rather recommended a highway above them. This would be a road of freedom from legalistic requirements but also a freedom from unbridled license and a giving way to every impulse of one's sinful nature. This is the ultimate meaning of a Spirit-led life. Such a person will check every wrong desire prompted by his evil nature and in this way he will fulfil the law. His moral and spiritual life has a freedom but also it has an integrity. This makes it impossible for the law to condemn or punish him.

The law is an alien principle, but when one is led of the Spirit he finds the will of God engraved in his heart in such a way that the flesh does not have dominating power over him. He becomes a whole personality and is under the willing and unresisted government of the Holy Spirit. The law would not have anything to forbid, because such a life would not desire forbidden things.

When one thus passes out of the dominion of the law, his heart is filled by the Spirit and he is living under the government of a new principle. He is no longer obedient to a formal law which is

cold and dead as a statue of stone, but there is within him a law
which possesses living power, fulfils itself in love and gradually
works out God's will in his personal life. Sin cannot have dominion
over him, for he is not under law but under the Spirit which has
been transmitted to him through God's grace.

4. Works of the Flesh (5:19–21)

5:19—The works of the flesh are manifest: To Paul, there was
a clearly defined standard by which one could decide whether he
was being led by the flesh or by the Holy Spirit. His list is concrete.
He enumerates the various manifestations and the inference is
that they are so plain and well known one does not need to be
reminded of the destructive force of them nor be urged to refrain
from their practice. Although we cannot be sure this list was con-
structed according to any definite pattern, it seems obvious they
fall into four divisions.

(1) Sins of sensuality, relating to one's sexual life. This includes
adultery, fornication, uncleanness, and lasciviousness.

(2) Sins related to perverted concepts of worship: idolatry and
witchcraft.

(3) Sins of the spirit caused by self-assertion and destructive of
fellowship and brotherhood. These include hatred, variance, emulations, wrath, strife, seditions, heresies, envyings, and murders.

(4) Sins related to self-indulgence: these include drunkenness
and revelings.

Adultery, fornication, uncleanness, lasciviousness: These first
four sins are related to the sexual conduct which was prevalent
in the cultic extravagances of the paganism of the Gentile world.
The Jewish people recoiled with horror from the moral degradation which, to them, had its rootage in the pagan ignorance of the
true God and the revelation he had given for man's moral guidance.

Judaism gradually influenced pagan moral and ethical thought,
but the attitude of the non-Jewish world toward these vices was
based on a strange concept. The pagan thinkers condemned an
action because of its antisocial character rather than because of
the violation of a God-given standard.

To them, fornication (which referred to illegitimate sexual relations in the widest sense of the word) was no more condemned

than self-indulgence with reference to food and drink. To them, it was a vice only when practiced beyond moderation. To the Jewish conscience, however, these sins were not merely against society but rather an affront to the God of character who had revealed himself in holiness and moral purity. There is no other area in which early Christianity so revolutionized the standards of the pagan world as in regard to sexual relationships. Although the King James Version has four words listed, in reality there are only three in the Greek manuscripts.

The first "fornication" originally referred to prostitution and was probably related to slaves who were bought to serve in that capacity. In biblical writings, however, the word means unlawful sexual relationships whether involving a violation of the marriage vows or not.

The word translated "uncleanness" was used by some of the earlier writers to refer to the uncleanness of a sore or a wound. Demosthenes used it with reference to moral depravity while in the Septuagint it is used of ceremonial impurity. The literal meaning seems to be "dirt" or "filth" with perhaps no special emphasis on sexual vice. But in the New Testament it stands often in association with the preceding word as denoting sexual impurity. Paul, no doubt, has in mind, in this context, the uncleanness of improper sexual relations.

The word translated "lasciviousness" is of doubtful etymology but was used by Greek authors to denote "wantonness" and "unrestrained wilfulness." Paul uses it elsewhere with words denoting sensuality (Rom. 13:13; 2 Cor. 12:21; Eph. 4:19). The fact that he groups it here with the other two words is a strong indication that it refers here to unrestrained indulgence in sexual relationships.

A final word is in order concerning the omission of "adultery" in modern translations. It seems clear that the King James Version translates a text which adds adultery to Paul's list.

5:20—Idolatry, witchcraft: These two words have to do with those practices characteristic of the pagan world's religion. They were entirely incompatible with spiritual religion as reflected in the purity of Hebrew monotheism. Many of the popular cults of that day were unashamedly purveyors of sexual immorality and gave such conduct open approval in the name of religion. God was merged into nature. The spiritual conception of deity was debased with fleshly attributes. There was no concept of man made in the image of God; rather the pagan world had made god in the likeness of corruptible man, birds, fourfooted beasts, and creeping things (Rom. 1:23). This word used for idolatry actually signified worship of images or false gods but in the heathen world idolatry and immorality were joined in an inseparable alliance. This particular word was also used to denote undue devotion to anyone or anything other than the true and living God (Eph. 5:5; Col. 3:5).

The Greek word *(pharmakeia)* translated "witchcraft" originally meant the preparation of medicines. From this developed the idea of the preparation and application of magical devices. When man has a low naturalistic concept of God he tries to operate upon it with material causes. This is the origin of magic. In such thinking natural objects were considered as possessing supernatural attributes. Thus the stars and even the flight of birds have divine omens ascribed to them. Drugs possessing mysterious power were credited with influence over the gods of nature. Since drugs were used in incantations and exorcisms, the Greek word *pharmakeia* came to mean "sorcery."

Today chemistry has destroyed this "world of magic" which existed in connection with the various herbs. It is easy now for us to understand how these superstitions were connected with sorcery and how witchcraft flourished under the various forms of idolatry. Superstitious dealings with the spirit world today are not too different from the preparation and application of magical devices in the pagan world of Paul's day.

5:20–21—Hatred, variance, emulations, wrath, strife, seditions, heresies, envyings, murders: These nine words all are concerned with the element of conflict in personal relationships. Although they are listed as part of the "sins of the flesh" they are in the truest sense "sins of the spirit." It is significant that they follow these other cataloged iniquities. Sins of fleshly indulgence always tear apart personal relationships.

It is impossible to build a community of goodwill among men if they have defied the very laws of purity and chastity which God has ordained as a part of his moral universe. There can be no brotherhood among men when there is indecency in sexual life. There may be superficial niceties expressed but such goodwill is shallow. Underneath it is greed and self-seeking. When the crisis comes, this personal ambition will manifest itself.

Personal rivalry and jealousy follow closely upon the heels of unbridled physical indulgences. The word translated "hatred" is the opposite in every respect of love *(agape)* and denotes enmity or hostility in whatever form it is manifested.

The word translated "variance" goes back to the classical Greek and occurs frequently in the history of the language. It has been translated rivalry, strife for prizes, fighting, discord, quarrel, wrangling, contention. It is used nine times in the New Testament—in every instance in letters of Paul.

The basic idea of this word is that of people choosing sides and each of the wranglers worshiping his hero. This word is used in 1 Corinthians 1:11 and 3:3 to describe the condition there because of the party factions. The word translated "emulation" is the Greek word *zalos* from which we get our English word "zeal." It is contrasted with the Greek word *phthonos* meaning "envy" and from this standpoint would be considered a "good word." Plato and Aristotle classed it as a "noble passion" but in the development of the language the "intense devotion" later became "anger" and later "jealousy" or "envy." It almost always arose out of devotion to another person or thing. It came also to mean the eager desire for possession created by viewing the properties of someone else. In this passage it is obvious the word is used in this last sense.

The word for "wrath" *(thumoi)* is plural and is a more passionate form of the word for "variance" *(eris)*. The word translated "strife" *(eritheiai)* may be rendered "factious cannibals" and is a stronger development of the word for "emulation" *(zelos)*. In *thumoi* we see "sowing emotions followed by explosions" while in *eritheiai* we have the etymology of a laborer for hire which then develops into "party spirit." *Thumos* has to do with "breath," "soul," "spirit," "heart." It is also related to "temper," "courage," "anger." In this particular passage it denotes a passionate outburst of hostile feeling. The best rendering of *eritheiai* (also plural) is "self-seeking," "selfishness," "factiousness," or "party spirit."

The next two words are the natural outgrowth of the others. The first, seditions *(eichostasiai,* plural), is a classical word, not found in the Septuagint, occurring only once in the Apocrypha and found only twice in the New Testament (here and Rom. 16:17).

The best translation is "dissensions." The Greek word *aireseis* (translated heresies) is a more aggravated form of the Greek word for seditions. It represents a further development. The divisions have now grown into distinct and organized parts.

The Greek word for envyings *(phthonoi)* means "ill-will," "malice," "envy," and is usually used in a bad sense except in James 4:5 where it is used for "eager desire for possession of" and refers to the Spirit of God. It is difficult in this Galatians context to separate it from *zalos* (zeal or emulation). If we are to differentiate, the first in the text would signify "jealousy" while the latter is best rendered "envyings." The plural, according to Burton, suggests "different acts, or specific forms of envious desire."

The word for "murders" is omitted in some of the ancient texts and is considered an interpolation from Romans 1:29 where this word and the one preceding it occur together. Lightfoot, however, argues for its authenticity and believes the omission in some texts may be due to the carelessness of the copyist transcribing words which so closely resemble each other. Actually, it makes good sense to leave this word in the text for the translation "murders" is the climax of the entire group of nine words dealing with schisms in personal relationships and attitudes. This word means more than merely a killing. It denotes murder. John Eadie says concerning this word, "the sudden or the deliberate sacrifice of any human life that stands in the way of self-advancement."

5:21—Drunkenness, revellings: These two words (*methai* and *komoi*) form the fourth group of vices which Paul names. They signify sins of indulgence where the spirit of unbridled license goes so far as to produce conduct that is degrading. While it is true, of course, that Paul is referring to repeated manifestations of intemperance we also should bear in mind that the Bible everywhere warns concerning the dangers of strong drink. The safest conduct with reference to alcoholic beverages is total abstinence. No one ever became an alcoholic who avoided the first drink. The word for "revellings" signified drinking parties.

Certain activity might begin with a band of friends accompanying a victor in an athletic contest. They would dance and laugh as they sang praises to him. It also referred to the devotees of Bacchus, the god of wine. Thayer speaks of a "nocturnal and riotous procession of half-drunken and frolicsome fellows who after supper parade through the streets with torches and music in honor of Bacchus or some other deity and sing and play before the house of their male and female friends; hence used generally of feasts and drinking parties that are protracted till late at night and indulge in revelry."

When we realize Christianity triumphed over this concept of life in the pagan world, we stand amazed at the power of the gospel and the dedicated courage of the apostles of that day.

And such like: Paul indicates here that his list is not exhaustive— merely suggestive. The "such like" refers to all of the seventeen "works of the flesh," not to the last one or two.

I tell you before, as . . . in time past: This means "I forewarn you" or "warn you beforehand." There is no doubt Paul must have instructed the Galatians during his previous visits both theologically and morally.

They which do such things: These Gentile churches were specially subject to these types of sins as indeed we are today. Who can say he is immune from temptation in this realm? The verb here *(prasso)* is the one for habitual practice not the one *(poieo)* for occasional doing. It is when this type of life become a habit that it is evident that the doer has not had a personal experience with Christ in forgiveness of sin, has not experienced the transforming power of the Holy Spirit, and is, therefore, not in the kingdom of God.

We have the same thought in 1 John 3:9: "Whosoever is born of God does not continue to practice sin for God's seed remains in him and he cannot continue to practice sin because he is born of God" (writer's translation).

5.   Fruits of the Spirit (5:22–23)

5:22—The fruit of the spirit: In cataloging the spiritual traits, Paul uses the singular in contrast to the plural in describing the "works of the flesh." This was in harmony with Paul's experience. In his pre-Christian days, while his sinful nature was rebellious toward God and at cross-purposes with its own self, his life had been fragmented into many compartments. With the coming of God's Spirit, he became an integrated personality living in fellowship with God and finding peace in the unifying love of Christ. Each fruit of the spirit was simply another form of the love of God which was revealed to him through Christ and interpreted to him through others who were committed to the Savior. If we attempt to divide these nine traits into various groups, we may do so as follows:

First, the basic spiritual qualities—love, joy, peace. Second, the virtues that show forth in our social relationships: long-suffering, gentleness, goodness. Third, the believers various relationships: faith or faithfulness (his relationship to God), meekness (his relationship with men), and his relationship to himself (temperance or self-control). Some, however, consider this an arbitrary and forced analysis.

Love: Volumes have been written concerning *agape* and its contrast to *eros* (physical passion) and *phileo* (humanitarian or brotherly love). This divine love is the root of all other graces. Paul said it was greater than faith and hope. All other graces are absorbed in it even as the flower is lost in the fruit. This is the love that is produced in the heart of one who has yielded to the Holy Spirit. It represents self-giving for the benefit of the one loved. It *becomes* because of a new and divine life which is implanted in the heart of the one who believes in Christ and commits himself fully to him. It is the foundation of the Christian life even as joy is the superstructure and peace is the crown.

Joy: This word expresses the spiritual gladness which has its basis in religious experience and whose real foundation is in fellowship with God. It is based on the possession of character and the opening up of a new world where dulness, despondency, and remorses are gone and the final hope of life is maturity and victory. This word does not mean the good feeling that comes from the possession of earthly things or cheap triumphs over someone in rivalry or competition. When true joy is present in one's life, there is the spring of boundless energy and the spontaneous praise whose instinctive dialect is a song of gladness.

Peace: This word means more than freedom from trouble. It includes everything that works for man's good and the realization of his highest ideals and ambitions. The Greek word, in the verb form, means to bind together. The theological implication is that Christ, through his atonement, binds together man and God who were separated because of sin. When one has the assuring consciousness that he is safe in the hands of God, there comes a tranquil serenity which pervades every part of his personality. This word, like the one preceding it, is a natural result of love. When one has peace in his heart, he has a desire to be an instrument in God's hand leading others to share this same tranquility. The peace-possessor will become a peacemaker. This is the word that translates the Jewish expression *shalom.*

Long-suffering: The Greek word used here dates back to the fourth century B.C. but occurs rarely in nonbiblical writers and only five times in the Septuagint or Apocrypha. It always conveys the same general idea—"steadfastness of soul under provocation to change." The word denotes endurance or forbearance. It also signifies bearing up under wrong without giving way to anger or seeking to avenge. In this context the probable meaning is forbearing those whose conduct would provoke one to anger. Chrysostom spoke of this grace as describing the man who "could revenge himself and who does not, or the man who is slow to wrath." The word is used often in the New Testament to express the attitude of God toward men. Rather than take his hand and destroy man, God has that quality which bears with man's sinning and will not cast him off. The word is not used very often in regard to things or events, but rather of patience and people.

Gentleness: This refers to the soft answer of a benign heart. It expresses a serene, loving, and sympathizing temperament. This virtue goes hand in hand with long-suffering as a mighty weapon against the hostility of the world in its attitude toward God's people.

Goodness: This word refers to that quality in a man who is guided by and aspires toward those things of moral worth. It is difficult to distinguish this term from the one preceding it. It suggests beneficence and may denote the actual manifestation of kindness as contrasted with the previous word which is more neutral. Lightfoot calls the former a "kindly disposition toward one's neighbors not necessarily taking a practical form" while he describes this latter word as "active . . . beneficence as an energetic principle." Trench points out that Jesus showed the first word (gentleness) when he was kind to the sinful woman who anointed his feet; but he showed the latter word (goodness) when he cleansed the Temple and drove out those who were making it a house of merchandise.

Faith: The Greek word used here may be translated faith or faithfulness. Actually, one is impossible without the other for faith makes it possible for one to be faithful. The word, however, does not seem to be used in the theological sense but with an ethical emphasis since the other words in this group have to do with matters of religious character.

Faith is, of course, the basic principle of life for one who is controlled by the Spirit, and thus it is impossible to separate these two concepts. Nevertheless, we seem to be more in the sense of the word when we see its passive meaning, trustworthiness, fidelity, honesty, etc., rather than the faith exercised by a person in order to secure salvation.

Included in this word is certainly the idea of confidence in God and all of his promises which produces a spirit of unsuspicious and generous confidence toward all people. Such a person will not be moved by doubts nor jealousies. He will not constantly be conjuring up possible causes of distrust in his fellowman. The secret of his faithfulness and service and his trusting attitude toward his fellowman goes back, of course, to his personal relationship with God. It was this "faithful faith" which steadied Paul in all the storms of his life and enabled him to walk on the highway of love which had been built by God who was faithful from the beginning and who loved us even when we were in rebellion to him.

5:23—Meekness: This English word usually indicates one who is humble in disposition and character. It suggests to our mind the idea of submitting without resistance when we are wronged. Thus the meek man is one who bears himself mildly and submissively in all things. Like a "weaned child" he neither accuses God nor does he attempt to avenge himself on man. These ideas are in the word, but there is an even more significant idea present. The meek man is the one who has a teachable spirit. He is willing to learn. The arrogant and self-assertive spirit refuses to admit the possibility there is something he does not know. A man's "teachableness" is the thing that sets him apart as a true disciple of Christ for the primary idea in being a disciple is that of learning. Those who "know it all" can never be a disciple of Christ. Likewise, it is the one who is constantly willing to be teachable who is more likely to mature in all of the Christian graces.

Temperance: The root meaning of the Greek word used here is "strong," able to master self. From this comes the idea of self-control, temperance, and even continence. The word certainly has reference to one's physical lusts in the realm of sex, but it is not limited to this meaning. Any bodily appetite or impulse is included, and the position of the word here in contrast to the works of the flesh probably suggests a special reference to the control of the appetite for strong drink and the resulting tendency to unrestrained and immodest behavior.

Temperance may well be described as a proper amount of the good things and total abstinence from evil things. Paul's self-control was not an attempt to induce a spiritual experience but rather the result of his fellowship with God. His rigid discipline, however, was very sane when compared with the indulgencies of the pagan or the ascetic excesses of some later Christian groups who forbade marriage and advocated fantastic rules of diet. As in all things, Paul advocated "sweet reasonableness" and consecrated common sense.

Against such there is no law: This phrase could be interpreted to mean "such things" or "such men" but in either sense the meaning is the same. We usually think of the law as negative and forbidding certain wrong actions. A more meaningful approach, however, is suggested here. When such virtues are practiced, it is a keeping or fulfilling of the law. Of course, only repentant sinners who have been transformed by the presence of Christ in their heart have a real appetite for the fruit of the spirit. Sometimes an unregenerate world, when it is exhausted with fighting and sick of its cynicism, has indicated a desire for spiritual things; but it is always on its own terms, which means without the atonement of Christ and the regenerating power of the Holy Spirit. No external law can compel men to produce any fruit of the spirit. These virtues come because of the overflow of God's love, as revealed in Jesus Christ, in the heart of the believer.

6. Essentials of Walking in the Spirit (5:24–26)

5:24—Have crucified the flesh: Paul has given a list of the Christian virtues. Now he gives the reason for this rich spiritual harvest. The believer has done to his old nature the same thing that was done to Christ on the cross. Paul could have used other words such as "die" or "abolish," but he chose the one that linked this total

change in attitude and conduct with the death of Christ. Those
who have accepted the crucified Savior should become in practice
what they are in principle. Man fell from his dignity through sin;
and the human spirit, when redeemed by Christ, is to assert mas-
tery over the flesh. Sinful yearnings and wicked cravings must be
brought completely under control of the love of Christ who died
for our sins and was raised for our justification.

Affections and lusts: Most Greek scholars suggest that the first
of these words refers more to a mental state and may be considered as passive in character. The latter represents desires that
have to do with active pursuit in gratifying those spheres which
are forbidden but to which the mind is ever prompted because
of its undeveloped and immature state.

5:25—Live in the Spirit . . . walk in the Spirit: This represents
an ideal state rather than an actual one. Paul is speaking of a way
of life to which the Galatians were committed because of their
having received Christ. When he said, "Live in the spirit," he
meant that this walk was implicit in their decision to become a
member of the Christian brotherhood, not that they had already
attained this goal. Since they have accepted this responsibility, it
now behooves them to make that profession a reality. The source
of their life is the Spirit. He must, therefore, direct their steps as
they advance step by step toward the goal of maturity. The only
way to deal with the passions and desires of the flesh is to destroy
them by the positive action of a Spirit-filled life.

5:26—Not desirous of vain glory, provoking . . . envying:
Wrong ambitions lead to the sin of putting false values on both
persons and things. The expression "desirous of vain glory" translates one Greek word having the idea of boasting without basis
which leads to pride and conceit. Such people have a haughty
attitude and contemptuous manner toward others and look upon
them with contempt. This causes hatred and produces a desire for
them to take revenge.

The legalistic attitude which had been fostered among the Galatians by the Judaizers would breed this kind of attitude. When
men base their Christian attainment upon the keeping of a code,
they automatically evaluate themselves by how well they perform
with reference to these individual items. They begin to swagger
and boast. This attitude provokes and challenges because one

becomes so eager to amount to more than the other. Each cannot stand the success of the other. Nonessentials are treated as matters of life and death and considered as proof that a person is superior to another. Competition and envy are not motivated by love and are not the fruit of a Spirit-filled life. Such an attitude lacks perspective and balance and causes one to lose the things that matter most—faith, hope, and love.

7.   Life in Christ Calls for Cooperative Attitudes and Action (6:1-6)

6:1—Brethren, if a man be overtaken in a fault: The chapter division here is unfortunate. The expression "brethren" does not represent a transition to a new train of thought. It actually points backward to the bickerings and wrong attitudes which the apostle spoke of in 5:26. Paul recognized the possibility that even one whose life is guided by the Spirit may stumble and fall into wrongdoing. The Greek word for "be overtaken" means literally "to take before another" or "to anticipate." This may indicate either that the person had been previously guilty or had recently fallen into temptation. In this context the latter is probably the correct sense in which the verb is to be understood. It has the idea of sudden temptation or a surprising action.

One who is born again does not deliberately plan to sin but may be tempted by Satan and yield because of impetuous or headstrong passions. Paul does not speak of restoring one who has a deliberate life pattern of sinning. The thrust of this passage is the picture of one who is the victim of a sudden temptation that has produced an unexpected lapse in the person's spiritual growth, not of a sinister person whose secret sin has been brought to light.

Ye which are spiritual: Some scholars believe Paul was speaking in a slightly sarcastic manner to those who were boasting of a superior spiritual attainment. They claimed to be superior—let them prove it. This word was chosen later by a group to designate themselves and the Gnostics associated this word with the "libertines" who considered themselves free from all restraints except the direct leadership of the Holy Spirit. It may be that at this time one of the parties in Galatia gave itself this title.

The most likely meaning, however, is that Paul was perfectly sincere and without bitterness or cynicism. He was paying them a compliment. He was speaking to them as people who had honestly sought to take his message to heart and be guided by the Holy Spirit. He was giving them credit for being mature, believing they were people who desired love and peace because they were walking in the Spirit and earnestly seeking to be men of goodwill. Furthermore, they were people who had not fallen into the same sins as the people whom they were urged to restore.

It is very necessary that those who would lead others to experiences with Christ should not be guilty of gross sins themselves. Those who wish to be leaders must exercise discipline in their own lives. Paul wrote to the Corinthians, "I keep under my body and bring it into subjection: lest that by any means, when I have preached to others, I myself should be a castaway" (1 Cor. 9:27). Such strict training is a part of spiritual growth. It is necessary if one would help restore others.

Restore . . . in the spirit of meekness: The verb used here has many meanings in the original language: to repair, to bring back to a useful condition, to complete. Kenneth Wuest says, "It is used of reconciling factions, of setting bones, of putting a dislocated limb into place, of mending nets, of manning a fleet, or supplying an army with provisions. It is used by Paul usually in a metaphorical sense of setting a person to rights, of bringing him into line." Paul's use of the word here is related to establishing a sinning brother and putting him back on the road to right living.

Any restoring process must, of course, begin with Christ, but our Lord always acts through individuals. Healing involves fellowship, and the task would not be complete until the one who has strayed is restored to the fellowship of believers. When the broken brotherhood has been reunited, the man once more becomes truly free and can in turn become a restorer for others who have fallen away from the fellowship.

Lest thou also be tempted: Far too often those who are morally weak in a certain area are prone to judge severely those who are guilty in that respect. Those who rise out of poverty are many times the harshest toward the poor. Is it because they desire to forget their past? Do they wish to escape any reminder of the condition in which they grew up and suffered? When a judge sentences someone severely who is guilty of an offense which tempts or has tempted him, is he trying to reinforce his own conscience and so give a warning to himself? There is some truth in this observation. Deeper Christian maturity, however, will cause us to be kind and compassionate toward those who are morally weak in any given direction. Paul practiced what he preached. The Galatians had actually erred grievously. It is true that he did not "whitewash" their sins but he did treat them gently and tenderly.

Perhaps the quality we need most, if we would be a restorer, is that of meekness. Christ was the "Good Shepherd" and Paul was "gentle as a nurse." Even when dealing with the worst offenders Paul preferred "to come in and love with the spirit of meekness" rather than "with a rod" (1 Thess. 2:7; 1 Cor. 4:21).

Religious zeal need not be harsh and overbearing. No person ever lived who was more zealous for God's work than Jesus of Nazareth. Yet he treated sinners with compassion. He dealt tenderly with those who had fallen. His bitterest words of condemnation were for those who failed to show kindness and understanding toward the weak and downtrodden.

A man is not capable of protecting himself against temptation. He needs God's Holy Spirit with him constantly as a guide and empowerer. He needs more than his own strength but, nevertheless, being watchful and sharply attentive is the first step in avoiding temptation. Accompanying this attitude, and just as necessary, is a sympathetic understanding of those who have fallen.

6:2—Bear ye one another's burdens: Common weakness produces sympathy. Paul passes from tolerance to active help. A Christian should do more than set a fallen brother on his feet. He should lend a helping hand so he will not stumble again.

There are many burdens which press a man down to defeat. In addition to wrongdoing, man is often bowed under the weights and fears of disappointment, anxiety, tension, weariness, and the plain pressures of everyday living. Personal infirmity, family difficulty, and business embarrassment drain one's personal resources. Anything that cripples a fellow Christian and hinders his running the race set before him should concern us. If we leave our friend to stagger alone and eventually sink under his load when we could have helped him by shouldering part of his burden, we are less than Christian and deserve reproach.

The Greek word used for "bear" may be translated endure,

suffer, carry, remove. It is the same word used in John 19:17 concerning Jesus, "And he bearing his cross went forth into a place called the place of a skull." Paul uses a different Greek word for "burden" in verse 5 where he refers to a burden which may be a good and legitimate one—a load of responsibility.

We should not forget, in considering verse 2, that Paul was writing to people who were inclined to put upon themselves legalistic burdens which God did not intend they should bear. This could add to their problem and increase their heavy load. When one helped them understand their freedom in Christ, he was helping them to shed some of their burden. (For fuller discussion of the difference between the two words for "burden," see comments on 6:5).

The law of Christ: Paul is not speaking of law in the legalistic sense of the word. He is rather referring to a life principle which has much deeper meaning than merely obedience to a set of rules. When one commits himself to follow Christ, he involves himself in what has been called "creative suffering." This means more than the absence of biting, devouring, and provoking one's brother. It means we shall love, help, and comfort him. We shall satisfy the requirements of Christlikeness only as we show concern for all of those who face the ravages of a cold and heartless world. Again, we should remember the Galatians were zealous to keep law—the law of Moses. Paul is giving them an even higher law to keep—the law of Christ. It is not done, however, in a legalistic way but with deeds of love and kindness motivated by the indwelling Spirit of God.

6:3—Think himself to be something . . . deceiveth himself: At first glance, this verse seems to hang loosely with the one preceding it. It is, however, vitally related to Paul's exhortation. The greatest hindrance to mutual burden-bearing is self-importance based on self-ignorance. If one imagines himself free of burdens or so above frailty, sorrow, or shortcomings that he shall never need help, he will be completely disinterested in helping others bear their burdens. Sympathetic concern makes us tender and generous. We shall be sympathetic and helpful toward others in direct proportion to our feeling weak and in need of assistance.

Paul does not mean we should belittle ourselves, not does he suggest that our attitude should be that we are completely unfit to perform any work for him. We must have a worthy opinion of ourselves, but we also must realize that any goodness or ability which we possess has been given us by God and is conveyed through Jesus Christ who infuses strength into us. Morbid self-contempt on the one hand is equally to be condemned with vain conceit on the other hand.

The people to whom Paul was writing, however, needed to be reminded more of the latter danger. Seeking to justify themselves by their legal deeds, they were in danger of exalting themselves with pride and insulating their lives from sharing the burdens of their weaker fellow Christians. This was self-inflation, self-deceit, and folly. They must be on guard against such arrogant self-esteem.

6:4—Prove his own worth: The true measure of our achievement is not by comparing ourselves with someone else. Such petty comparisons may feed our vanity, but they are of no avail when we stand in the presence of a completely holy God. Honesty enables, indeed requires, us to see we are nobody. The doctrine of justification by faith in Christ, apart from works of the law, brings home to us forcefully our own inadequacies. If we study our brother's work, it should be to help him do better—not in order to rationalize our own superiority. When we use the faults of others as a norm for evaluating ourselves, we are opening up many avenues of wrong thinking.

There is the temptation to deal with ourselves too gently in the mirror of another person's conduct and eventually to become puffed up with pride because of our own accomplishments. It is God who is our judge. He will accept our intrinsic goodness not our comparative goodness. We should never indulge in vain imaginations but bring our work to a true and honest test in the light of God's requirements. If we ever attain any degree of success, we shall be so humble because we have still fallen short of God's standard that we will give him the praise and the glory for it all.

True Christian maturity never finds any measure of satisfaction in outstripping another in good deeds. Paul's exhortation does not exclude the possibility that we may find approval because of our righteous acts, but it will not be on the basis of climbing over our fellow Christians in a mad race to find favor with God.

6:5—Shall bear his own burden: Lightfoot contends it is difficult to distinguish precisely between the two words for "burden" in verse 2 and verse 5. Thayer renders the one in verse 2 *(baros)* as meaning heavy in weight, burdensome, severe, stern, violent, cruel, unsparing, while the one in verse 5 *(phortoin)* is "burden" in the sense of "load." He gives as an illustration "the freight or lading of a ship." Thus "burden" in verse 2 is one which he may rid himself of with proper help but the one in verse 5 is the kind of load he is expected to bear in life's ordinary pursuits. It is often used as the word for a man's pack or a soldier's kit supplied with his own provisions which he is expected to bear. Thus in verse 5 Paul is speaking of a Christian's ordinary obligations. He must bear these himself. In verse 2 he speaks of the "over burden" of oppressive weight.

No man can escape his normal duty, but if Christian friends help him with his extra weights he can find relief. Thus life is both a solo and a chorus. Certain responsibilities are ours. We must accept them. On the other hand, Christian fellowship requires that we "share our mutual woes and our mutual burdens bear." One cannot refrain from believing that, in the paradoxical nature of these two verses, Paul is also saying it is not the burdensome ritual of the law that he wants to see them bear but rather the errors, weaknesses, sorrows, and sufferings of your neighbor (see comments on 6:2).

6:6—Him that is taught . . . him that teacheth: This verse is a transition statement. Paul has been speaking of correct conduct toward erring brethren. He balances his exhortation with a statement concerning proper treatment of teachers.

First, Paul dealt with our attitude toward inferiors whom we are tempted to despise and then spoke in this verse of our attitude toward superiors whom we are prone to neglect. If one is guilty of one, he is in danger of ill treatment of the other. If one is harsh in treating the weak, he is apt to show rudeness and insubordination toward the strong. When one is self-conceited and self-sufficient, he is apt to show a cold contempt toward his inferiors and a jealous independence of those above him. A proper realization of our weaknesses will make us treat our inferiors correctly; and a proper sense of our obligation to God will make us deal properly with those who teach us.

The phrase under consideration may indicate there was already a highly developed catechetical system in the churches of Galatia, but most scholars doubt such formal instruction exited on a large scale this early. There may have existed a "teaching elder" in each church (1 Tim. 5:17). If such a person existed, had great authority, and were guilty of the Judaizing heresy, he could have been a dangerous person. More probably, however, Paul is speaking of the Christians in general as those who are being taught in the word rather than a special select class under the tutelage of a specific leader. The verse is a "bridge verse" between the injunction to treat weaker Christians correctly and the warning concerning sowing and reaping which follows in the next three verses.

Communicate . . . in all good things: The Greek word used for the verb here means literally to have in common, to share, to be associated in. From this comes the idea of "to communicate with" in the way of aid and relief. The meaning is clear. Jesus expressed it, "the labourer is worthy of his hire" (Luke 10:7). This phrase, however, has a larger scope than merely referring to material things.

A true minister of Christ works for unity among the brethren and seeks cooperation from all types of people within the congregation. Unless he has this, his work will be weak and unsuccessful. The pastor should not be left to bear all the burdens, fight all the battles, and accept all the responsibilities in the local church. There should be a sympathetic union and an equitable division of work between "him that is taught" and "him that teacheth" so God's work may be strengthened.

In a congregation, it is the fellowship of a unified spirit that knits together the members into a beautiful unity to God's glory and to the advancement of his work in a community. One cannot "pay the preacher" and then feel all his duties to God or even to the pastor are performed. It is important to support the ministry with money (too few people are faithful in this regard), but the giving of money is a spiritual act and when done properly will overflow into other areas of concern for the one who teaches. A wise pastor teaches his people the importance of bringing their money to support God's work. He knows that when their money is dedicated to Christ's work they will be more interested in kingdom service. Jesus did not say, "Where your heart is your treasure will be." He rather declared, "Where your treasure is there will your heart be also" (Matt. 6:21). How well Jesus understood human nature!

8.   The Law of the Harvest (6:7–10)

6:7—Be not deceived; God is not mocked: Paul is about to introduce a great spiritual principle but he precedes it with a solemn warning lest we neglect the truth of it. Surely no one could argue with the law of harvest in the fields and orchards. Everyone even incidentally associated with farming knows that like produces like in the realm of agriculture. In the realm of the moral and ethical, however, we are not quite so ready to remember that this rule works. One's character is actually the harvest of his habits.

Why is it we fail to remember this truth in its broader application? Perhaps it is because good and bad often seem strangely mingled. It is often difficult to say that a man is either one or the other. Paul insists, however, that the very character of God himself is at stake in the affirmation and even insistence upon the working out of moral law. Fallen creatures are unstable and capricious. God must not be identified with such lack of consistency. We are guilty of blind conceit when we imagine anyone can escape from the stern regularity of God's moral government.

When we violate moral laws, we inevitably face moral deterioration. We may not observe it immediately; but harvest will arrive in due time because God is sovereign and, therefore, in complete charge of every area of his created universe. Because it is law-governed, it reflects the mind of its Creator as surely as a mirror reflects the physical image of the one gazing into it.

Whatsoever a man soweth, that shall he also reap: This "law of recompense" works with automatic and inexorable exactitude. It is a fundamental principle of life and cannot be ignored. Man cannot hoodwink God nor evade the laws by which he governs the universe. When God gave believers the Holy Spirit, he presented them a new standard and a new motive power. This was to guide all areas of living but especially their relationships with their fellowmen. This cause and effect law in human character serves as a basis for all moral responsibility.

Man's future destiny is related intimately to his present choice. The harvest is bound up inextricably with the sowing that is practiced here and now. It is the quality rather than the mere quantity in which we find a strict agreement with the sowing. Many times the harvest surpasses the seed by thirty, sixty, or a hundred fold. In degree there may be an infinite difference, but in kind the harvest is exactly the same. This truth has its counterpart in the moral realm.

The way in which one hears the gospel and its implicit claims and then reacts to them determines the eternal destiny and to a large extent the type of life one experiences while still in the flesh. Eternal life lies within embryo at faith's earliest beginning when it is still but "a grain of mustard seed." The final outcome is, of course, an intensification of all that has entered into one's body and spirit in the various duties and disciplines of life.

6:8—Soweth to his flesh: The general principle outlined in the previous verse is developed in two directions. If one gives rein to passion and the satisfying of physical appetite, the harvest will reflect this choice. Every selfish and pleasure-seeking act weakens the soul's life.

If one is selfish, he degenerates into sensuality. From sensuality one plunges downward into the bottomless pit. When man's natural passions are unsubdued and uncleansed, they breed corruption and death. One's soul can rot in his body when lust and greed eat out of him all capacity for good. We can tell what has been going on within a man when we see his bloated face, sensual leer, vicious eye, and sullen brow. Licentiousness and intemperance make up an offensive disease. When a person yields to it, he will find a bitter harvest overtaking him probably in this world and certainly in the world to come.

The entire concept of hell is that which is debasing and corrupting. Sensuality's harvest is degradation and defilement. False religions appeal to man's fallen nature. They satisfy his religious instinct but permit him to continue in personal sin. The Judaizers were catering to the lower nature of the Galatians when they ignored or at least minimized regeneration and stressed a "salvation-by-works religion." They glorified man rather than God. This is prone to allow man a continuation of his personal sins while he is endeavoring to buy God's favor by the performance of certain ritual. Paul's contention was that this would only add to corruption in their personal lives. He indicates in chapter 5 that this corruption was already beginning in the lives of the Galatians.

Paul is speaking of more than "sowing wild oats" and reaping them. He is speaking of a physical and moral decay that comes because one is living within the realm of sin and death rather than in the realm of life in Christ Jesus.

Soweth to the spirit: Unbridled and defiant conduct becomes its own penalty, but the life created by God's Holy Spirit through oneness with Christ has no interruption nor conclusion. Our immortality comes from living union with Him who defeated death. Such a relationship means the best of this world *and* blessedness in the world to come.

There is nothing wrong in looking for a reward both here and hereafter. Such a hope is not an "opiate" of the masses but it is intrinsically the natural outcome of right living. When one's affections are healthy, he finds happiness in this world. When we have learned to love the acceptance of responsibility, we find the joy in life that is unsurpassed by any type of lower living.

Included in this sowing to the spirit is, quite obviously, the forgiveness of Christ. This involves healing and cleansing one's emotions and the saturation of one's personal life with Christ's quality of mind. Inner resources, like a well of water springing up daily, will bring cleansing, healing, and renewing of our emotional life and every attitude that saturates our personality.

The greatest promise of the New Testament is life. When spiritual life begins in a man, it progressively expels the evil things within him. It becomes more and more alive as the days pass. The harvest of everlasting life has a special reference to heaven but we must not limit it to the life beyond the grave. The life which is bestowed on a believer who is daily sowing good seed is enjoyed in this present life as well. The fruit of a good conscience, unselfish life, and a heart dedicated to high ideals is the "peace that passeth all understanding" which Paul promises will guard our hearts and minds. This, as well as heaven, is the life offered to the spiritually oriented.

6:9—Let us not be weary in well doing: This means literally "doing that which is beautiful" and is a very comprehensive concept. It implies helping anyone who is in need of anything—physical sustenance or spiritual guidance. It is the weakness of our human nature which constantly prevents our continued effort at a task. We are prone to love ease, lack staying power, and become discouraged. When we do not see visible results immediately,·the temptation is to lose heart and give up. If friends refuse to cooperate as we feel they should, it is easy for our idealism to become sour and produce frustration or even cynicism. The verb for "be weary" has within it the idea of fainthearted, or lose courage in the course of action.

Paul uses this same word in 2 Thessalonians 3:13 and 2 Corinthians 4:1, while Jesus is recorded as using this word when he said that "men ought always to pray and not to faint" (Luke 18:1).

In due season: If we believe in God's sovereignty, we must believe that the time for our vindication is with him. If the time of labor appears long and the crop seems to grow slowly, we must remember that, because he is Judge, he has control of the seasons. When it is time to harvest the crop, he will say, "Thrust in thy sickle and reap." We shall enjoy the fruit of our work if we do not relax our efforts and become exhausted physically, spiritually, or emotionally. We must keep ever alive the incentive to stay on the job and never slacken our activity in things of the Spirit. The "weary mood" is never far from us but it must be watched or it will overtake us.

We, in our spiritual life, are, as the farmer, in league with mighty and mysterious forces. God's presence fills the dim background. He is the great Ally on the field. Our methods and implements of work are but reverent leagues and covenants with him. Paul told the Philippians to "work out your own salvation" but immediately reminded them, "It is God that worketh in you."

God's heartening promise is that he is Lord of the moral harvest as well as the physical one. The order and regularity of nature finds its counterpart in the moral and spiritual world. We must never be disappointed in the slowness of harvest but must remember that in the spiritual sphere there are no casualties; no room for accidents or failure. Every law partakes of God's absoluteness.

As the divine chemistry of nature regulates the tiny germ in the soil until it becomes a lovely flower, so God's grace will guarantee that the smallest seeds of goodness in a human heart will produce a glorious harvest which will make this life happier and heaven richer.

6:10—As we have therefore opportunity: There are two words for "time" in the Greek language. One *(chronos)* means "time generally or in the abstract." The other *(kairos)* means the proper season or right time for any action. From this comes the idea of a seasonable time or opportunity. Paul, of course, uses the latter word in this context.

Let us do good unto all men: This entire section has, underlying it, the concept of doing good. Paul speaks of restoring a fallen brother, bearing one another's burdens, sharing with one's teacher in material possessions, and untiring service. In this verse Paul seems to sum up all of these virtues in one vivid exhortation. It includes all that has gone before and even adds an implication for complex varieties in all social duties. Whatever obligation may arise in immediate form—kindness, beneficence, or mercy—and whether the duty is temporary or spiritual, one should do "the good thing" as the opportunity arises.

Paul constantly urges perseverance in good works as a fruit of grace. The word "all" suggests, even demands, that this service should be rendered to anyone no matter who they are or where they are. Our Lord's active love leaped over various barriers and boundaries and his servants should do no less. No one lives as an isolated unit. We are bound together in a bundle of life and have obligations to one another.

Especially unto them . . . of the household of faith: Paul is not qualifying what he has just said. He is rather enforcing a specific application. This phrase does not at all minimize Paul's belief in the universality of the gospel message. It is rather to recognize that those who are born again constitute a redeemed family, and there are certain privileges and responsibilities in a family relationship. A person is not likely to be really concerned about the needs of others if he ignores those in his own family. An insincere person can avoid local and legitimate responsibility by feigning a concern for the nebulous and far-off.

A person who is not interested in the non-Christian near him is not really concerned about the lost person in faraway places. Those who are near to us have a peculiar claim upon us. They who share our common faith deserve special attention from us in their time of need. Fellow believers form a distinct family and it is not unchristian to recognize this in our deeds of kindness and service.

Conclusion
6:11–18

The letter is now finished. Paul has made his final appeal for patience and continuity in the Spirit-filled life. He wishes to reaffirm, in summary, the main emphases of the letter. It may be that he took up the pen himself at this point and added the few final words with his own hand.

1.   Paul's Own Hand in Writing (6:11)

6:11—How large a letter . . . with mine own hand: Some scholars see here an indication that Paul wrote this entire letter himself —without any scribal assistance. This has been a rather popular, view through the years. Other scholars, however, have pointed out some difficulty in this interpretation. The expression "how large a letter" is more accurately translated "with large letters."

It has been suggested rather strongly by many scholars that Paul picked up the pen himself at this point in order to add a personal touch with his own hand. He wished to summarize the main parts of the letter with the utmost possible emphasis and even solemnity. He wanted to imprint them as indelibly as he knew how upon the heart and soul of the Galatians. He began by calling attention to the big letters he was using. This was in order to impress the readers and drive home the importance of the last section he was writing with his own hand. It is true he used the aorist tense for the verb which indicates completed action but this was in accordance with Greek custom known as the "epistolary aorist." He was associating himself with his readers. As they read it, it would be correct that Paul "has written" the thing they are now reading.

Of course, it must be pointed out that there are still scholars today who do not accept this modern school of thought. They contend strongly the entire letter was written in Paul's own handwriting. Kenneth S. Wuest admits that six of the seven best au-

137

thorities he has studied maintain Paul wrote only the conclusion
but he insists Paul wrote the entire letter in the cursive style. He
insists the epistolary aorist is never used in the New Testament
with reference to something about to be written. He calls attention to the fact that 2 Thessalonians 3:17, which is an example of
Paul adding his own personal salutation with his own hand, contains the present tense. Why would not Paul have used the present
tense in Galatians as in the Thessalonian letter?

Why did Paul write in large letters? Wuest insists Paul had
contracted an Oriental eye disease called opthalmia which made
him almost totally blind. Why did Paul write the entire letter?
Wuest insists it was in order to have the most personal touch
possible with the Galatians under the circumstances.

There is no theological problem involved in whether or not Paul
wrote all of the letter by hand or merely the last part. One can
study the evidence and reach his own conclusion.

2.   Circumcision Contrasted with the Cross (6:12-15)

6:12—Desire to make a fair show in the flesh: The Gentiles
would probably not understand this statement. To them this was
probably considered a disfiguring custom resembling the tattoo-
ing of savages. Paul considered the Judaizers as desiring "ecclesias-
tical statistics"—so many circumcisions in a given year!

In the flesh: This does not refer to fleshly things nor even to the
idea of among or before men. It rather denotes the sphere
wherein the "showy" appearance manifests itself. The unregenerate nature is implicit in the use of flesh and is particularly
related to this special aspect of sensuousness and externalism. This
was an area in which the flesh opposed the spirit in both principle
and result. As they lusted in fleshly things, they canceled all of the
virtues of justification by faith. This developed into selfishness,
questionable moral acts, and severed those related to it from the
"fruit of the spirit." They were far away from "crucifying the
flesh" but rather they found great glory in magnifying and exalting
it.

Lest they should suffer persecution for the cause of Christ: What
was the true motive of the Judaizers in exerting such a moral
compulsion upon the Gentile Christians to be circumcised? It was
to compensate for having left the Jewish faith. It was an effort to

have the best of both sides. The orthodox Jews felt great resentment toward those who had left the faith to accept Jesus of Nazareth as the Messiah. The Judaizers wanted to escape their enmity by insisting on circumcising the Gentile converts. This was a way of showing the orthodox Jew they had not deserted the law. They had required all members of the Christian church to observe it and thus had carried Jewish influence into spheres of society which could not normally be reached by the synagogue.

Paul suffered great persecution because he had insisted that Christ's death on the cross freed the believer from any obligation to Judaism. He was not against the law but he was against the bondage of required observance of the rituals and ceremonies of the law. Paul's life in Christ produced a higher morality and a purer motive than the law ever brought to an individual. Nevertheless, he suffered great persecution from the Jews who would not accept Christ. The Judaizers, on the other hand, wished to escape that persecution by presenting a respectable figure when they confronted Jews who had not even nominally accepted Christ.

6:13—They themselves who are circumcised: There is a difference of opinion among scholars as to whether this phrase refers to those Gentiles who were becoming circumcised at the insistence of the Judaizers or the Judaizers themselves. Of course, Paul could be referring to both groups. There is no real theological point involved. His emphasis seems to be upon the insincerity of this group which leads us to think he is referring to the Judaizers.

Neither . . . keep the law: To what law is he referring? It is true, of course, that in the fullest sense of the word no one keeps the law. We all have come short. It is doubtful Paul is speaking of the fact that they are not observing the sacrificial law or even joining in the numerous observances of the Jewish nation. It is rather their insincerity which is revealed by the lack of true compassion. Jesus, in the days of his flesh, spoke of the Jews who "bind heavy burdens and grievious to be borne, and lay them on men's shoulders; but they themselves will not move them with one finger" (Matt. 23:4). He declared that they "have made the commandment of God of none effect by your tradition" (Matt. 15:6). His point was that they contrived devious means and subterfuges in order to circumvent the true intention of the law. It was perhaps in this sense that Paul is speaking. It is so easy to rationalize!

That they may glory in your flesh: Even today the soul-winner must be careful lest he is guilty of feeding his own ego through his converts. Although the "communication of truth through personality" is a great definition of preaching, we do not dominate people with an overpowering personality and thus lead them into a personal experience with Jesus as Savior and Lord. We must be winsome and use every kind and loving approach available but when our converts cause an unhealthy pride within us, something is wrong with our evangelistic efforts. As in all things, there is a point of "sweet reasonableness" and no one can completely eliminate a justifiable pride in successfully leading a person to become a Christian. Motivation must constantly be analyzed. Paul was convinced the people who were disturbing the Galatians were acting in a role which was other than sincerely Christian.

6:14—God forbid that I should glory: The literal Greek reads, "But for me may it not be that I should glory." Paul places the first phrase in a position of emphasis in order to contrast himself with those of whom he has just spoken. The expression translated "God forbid" is an idiom. Paul uses it several times in the New Testament in order to declare his horror at, or repugnance to, some teaching or action. Other renderings have been "Perish the thought!" and "Let it be flung from us as an abominable thing!" (See comments on 2:17 and 3:21.)

In the cross of our Lord Jesus Christ: Since Paul took such a strong stand against circumcision, it would be natural to expect him to glory or "boast" in uncircumcision. He found, however, no particular value in either state (see v. 15). His only ground of boasting was the cross of Jesus Christ. By this, of course, he does not mean the literal piece of wood but rather the act performed on the cross when the God-man was crucified.

To Paul, the cross made all the distinctions among mankind meaningless. It breaks down completely our connection with the things of the outward world. It gives all men, irrespective of nationality, a new outlook. Man no longer looks at things from a human point of view but rather he evaluates his fellowman, and the moral and spiritual issues of the world, from the standpoint of God's outlook. The cross was the last thing which natural man would ever have chosen as a reason for boasting. To the Jew (legalistic mind), the cross was a stumbling block while to the Greeks (the philosophical mind) it was sheer foolishness.

People who are seeking to be justified by their own deeds, whether the Judaizers of the first century or their modern counterparts, will always stumble when they come face to face with the atoning work of Christ and are urged to put their complete faith in the act of this Person for redemption. Likewise, sophisticated pride which imagines itself to be highly intellectual regards a substitutionary death as "ridiculous" and refuses to consider it for even a moment as a way of salvation. Christ's death on the cross exposes man's desperate state. It points out the fact that he is utterly bankrupt in the moral and spiritual realm. The sufferings of Christ reveal the folly of all human pride and cause man to see and confess his own worthlessness.

The world is crucified unto me, and I unto the world: At first glance, this seems like redundancy. At second glance, it might be considered as Hebrew parallelism. Actually, however, there are two separate meanings, although it must be admitted they are very closely interrelated. First, "the world had become dead to Paul." The Holy Spirit had worked in him a complete transformation. The pleasures and treasures the world had to offer had completely lost their charm and attractiveness for Paul. Likewise, various honors conferred upon men by worldly people had no appeal for the apostle.

The second phrase indicates that "Paul had become dead to the world." This means the world no longer attempted to attract Paul. This could mean that worldly people treated him as an object of contempt and recognized the futility of any attempt to attract him and draw him away from Christ. There also may be the suggestion of a personification of the world. This personified personality had the same attitude as literal individuals. They had nothing to do with Paul. They were disgusted with him because he had positionized himself with Christ and rejected the claim of the world completely.

One scholar expressed it this way, "Paul's ideals and outlook have now become so spiritual and unworldly that the world can ignore him just as though he had ceased to be." This has been called the "discipline of the cross," but we must understand that this is not another form of law. It has nothing to do with any effort to earn the grace of God through good works.

This discipline rather puts its pressure upon the man who is already a new creature because of his experience with Christ. He has new insights, methods, and power which enable him to grow in the Christian life. Evil has been destroyed within him without destroying him as a person. The discipline of the cross does not violate his freedom but makes him even more free because he is more like Jesus. It is one's union with the Crucified One that makes such a life possible. It is more than a duty to be performed in life. It is a glorious privilege—that of fellowship with the living Christ because one has become dead to those things which are in opposition to Jesus and his way of life.

6:15—In Christ Jesus: Few people have ever possessed the ability of Paul to grasp the entire concept of what it means to be a Christian. Perhaps the most meaningful expression is that of a "mystical union" with him which results in a vital fellowship. In 2:21 Paul said, "Christ liveth in me" (see comment on this verse). Paul saw no contradiction whatsoever in saying that he lived "in Christ" and that Christ "lived in him." The two were wedded together in an indissoluble spiritual amalgamation.

Neither circumcision . . . nor uncircumcision, but a new creature: To Paul, being a Christian was many things. It was "passing from death unto life," becoming a "purchased possession," and "being justified by faith." Here, however, is one of the noblest concepts. The Christian is a new creation. The main message of the New Testament is that in Jesus we can be made anew.

In the death and resurrection of Christ, we have a fresh spiritual energy which can conquer us and make us, in turn, conquerors over the evil past which has held us in its clutches. Man is more than a piece of physical machinery that will endure for a certain span of time. He is a soul within a body. God's love in Jesus can transform him inwardly and cause him to express himself outwardly in a new way of life. This new birth was not related to either circumcision nor uncircumcision nor to any act of obedience. It was rather the experience in Christ which produced the desire and motivation to become obedient.

The real difference between a Christian and a non-Christian is that the former has been created anew in Christ Jesus and activated by his love. Paul had discovered that circumcision could not automatically guarantee a man would love his neighbor or bear his neighbor's burdens. It was only a personal experience with Jesus in forgiveness of sin that set the spiritual climate for the transforming work of the Holy Spirit to make one new in Christ.

3. Final Prayer and a Concluding Challenge (6:16–17)

6:16—Walk according to this rule: Paul is referring here to the principle he has enunciated in the previous verse but, no doubt, also has in mind the "discipline of the cross" mentioned in verse 14. The one who is a new creation in Christ is indeed glorying in nothing but the cross for this is the means of his redemption and the basis of his transformation.

A person is a new creature when he places his complete and unqualified trust in the crucified Savior and regulates his life by this principle. He will be grateful and produce Christian service out of his love for the Savior, not because he thinks God attaches significance to earthly externals among which is circumcision.

When Paul spoke of rule, he was not thinking of a set of do's and don't's nor any static test of morality. He had one great goal—to lift his readers above the level of legalistic righteousness. This rule was rather a comprehensive understanding of everything the apostle has said in his letter. It is the reflection of a new norm and a new measure in living. Its departure was the cross of Christ and the new creature in Christ is the fulness of its realization. Everything must be tested by this standard. It is the mind of Christ which serves as the touchstone by which we consider as valid the choices of our life or reject them as unworthy of the Christian way.

Walk: This verb means "to advance in a line" and from this we get the idea of "to direct one's life" or "frame one's conduct." George Findlay suggests the apostle is thinking of the "measured, even pace, the steady march of the redeemed host of Israel." The idea is of those who are moving forward to make spiritual maturity the goal of their endeavors.

Peace . . . and mercy: These two go together. They have been compared to the pillar of fire and cloud in the wilderness. Paul places the result first probably because he wishes to emphasize it as being the distinctive and provident gift of God. Peace brings a serenity of heart to all who have been justified by faith in Christ.

It is spiritual completeness.

The two terms are inseparable for if God had not shown mercy to his people they would be incapable of possessing peace. Yet one thing should be noted about peace. There is a "peace with God" (Rom. 5:1), but there is a "peace . . . which passeth all understanding" (Phil. 4:7) which Paul says "shall keep your hearts and minds through Christ Jesus." The first peace comes in justification. The second comes in Christian growth and maturity. Every believer has the "peace with God" but it is in proportion to our Christian growth that we have the "peace . . . that passeth all understanding." It is the second peace that Paul is speaking of in this verse. Any peace which man possesses is, of course, because of God's mercy. Backslidings are healed and daily sins are forgiven because of God's mercy as much as man is justified in the initial experience of salvation by his mercy.

The Israel of God: Paul makes it clear elsewhere (3:29, see also Rom. 2:28–29) that the true Israelite is the Christian. He has inherited the spiritual promises made to Abraham. Paul makes it clear elsewhere that "they are not all Israel, which are of Israel" (Rom. 9:6) which is certainly in harmony with calling Christian people "the Israel of God." An outstanding Jewish evangelist who was converted to Christianity insisted on saying, "I am not a 'converted' Jew. I am a 'completed' Jew." Christianity is the full flower of Judaism and they who are in Christ are the true spiritual heirs of him to whom it was promised: "In thee shall all the families of the earth be blessed" (Gen. 12:3).

6:17—From henceforth let no man trouble me: Paul feels he has vindicated himself personally. His conscience is unruffled and serene. Since he is loaded down with many responsibilities, he feels he should be granted immunity from any future problems—especially of the type caused by the Judaizers. It requires energy to "set people straight" and this exhausts the one who is assigned the task. It is with deep feeling that he demands to be spared the distress his opponents had been inflicting upon him. He wants to give his best, in the future, to the missionary work to which God has called him. He does not want to be disturbed by petty people with selfish ambitions. Paul never asked to be excused from hard work, but he does wish to be free from annoyances that drain his energy which should be put to more constructive work. This same phrase is used in Mark 14:6 and Luke 11:7 by Jesus to indicate the giving of inconvenience or even trouble. This strong statement by Paul is perhaps indirectly an assertion once more of his apostolic authority. He must be free to do the work to which God has called him.

Bear in my body the marks of the Lord Jesus: There is no doubt Paul is referring to his physical sufferings and perhaps actual scars. This figure of speech is an interesting one. Some scholars have suggested he was referring to a custom spoken of in Herodotus by which a fugitive took refuge in a temple and received upon his body the marks of the pagan god. After this, he could not be touched. Other scholars have pointed out that marks were put on a soldier indicating the general under whom he was serving. While both of these represent possibilities, there is no doubt the custom of marking slaves was familiar to both Paul and the Galatians.

The most accepted interpretation, therefore, is that Paul was thinking of himself as a slave and referring to the marks which were always present upon a slave designating the master's ownership. The concept of slave to master is one of the most meaningful in the New Testament.

Alexander Maclaren says, "It is the most uncompromising assertion of the most absolute authority on the one hand, and claim of unconditional submission and subjection on the other." Such a relationship between man and man is atrocious and blasphemous but when this is described as the relationship between a redeemed man and Jesus Christ, his Redeemer, it is one of the most magnificent truths to be found anywhere. It is the basis for the doctrine of the lordship of Christ which calls for our complete surrender to him in every area of our life. Obedience is to be absolute, unquestioning, and unreserved. We belong completely and unconditionally to the one who has purchased us through his great redemptive act on Calvary.

4. A Benediction (6:18)

6:18—Brethren: This letter has been one of reproof and strenuous exhortation. By using this word at the close it does much to soften the rebuke and, most of all, to express Paul's continued affection for the Galatians. Paul uses the term frequently in his letters but no other time does he add it as a concluding benediction.

The grace of our Lord Jesus Christ: This both summarizes and presupposes everything which Christ is able to bestow to the believer. The word "grace" implies the blessing as unearned and undeserved. Paul seems to be using here a shortened form of the trinitarian formula which occurs in 2 Corinthians 13:14. It is not fair to say the shorter form is less rich but it may be that the richness is not as fully expressed as in the longer form. The brevity of this benediction may reflect the tension under which Paul wrote this particular letter.

An in-depth consideration of these words, however, reveals Paul's concluding blessing pronounced upon them lacks nothing in beauty and meaning. He concentrates upon grace as that which sustains and equips the believer to be a living witness and enables one to have the peace that passes all understanding. He specifically mentions Jesus and gives him his full title.

It is also significant that Paul's farewell greeting to the churches of Galatia was almost identical with that to the one at Philippi whom he described as "beloved and longed for, my joy and my crown . . . beloved" (Phil. 4:1).

With your spirit: True religion moves one's entire inner being. When we are informed of the reality of God through his grace, we are moved to put our trust in him and conduct ourselves according to the revelation we have received. This produces a change within us. Our spirit bears testimony with his Spirit. We are thus able to experience joy abounding because of the presence of Christ within. It is when our religion moves from the external to the internal that we learn the joy of spiritual fellowship with Christ.

As long as we are human, we have a need for certain external "crutches" to assist us but as we mature in the faith our religion becomes more vital as it becomes inward and spiritual. The spirit is the higher nature. It is the region in which the divine operates in both the new birth and continued growth and maturity.

Amen: The apostle brings this remarkable letter to a close with strength and depth of feeling. It was written under the stress of deep emotion and probably was dictated very rapidly. It, nevertheless, constitutes one of the most important monograms of his day or any day. There is a strong plea for Christian liberty which, at the same time, cautions against excessive license. Paul seeks to conserve the best of all the past.

He believes we are heirs of yesterday, but we must move in today's freedom across the threshold to a bright tomorrow. This can be done only one way—by a personal relationship with Christ based on faith and producing a vital fellowship which maintains self-discipline but, at the same time, thinks creatively, lives constructively, and rejoices triumphantly. To all of this that Paul taught, we, too, can shout a glorious "Amen!"

Bibliography

BARCLAY, WILLIAM. *The Letters to the Galatians and Ephesians*. 2d ed. ("The Daily Study Bible.") Philadelphia: The Westminster Press, 1958.

BARNES, ALBERT. *II Corinthians and Galatians*. ("Notes on the New Testament.") Grand Rapids: Baker Book House, n.d.

COLE, R. A. *The Epistle of Paul to the Galatians*. Grand Rapids: Wm. B. Eerdmans Publishing Co., 1965.

DUNCAN, GEORGE S. *The Epistle of Paul to the Galatians*. ("The Moffatt New Testament Commentary.") London: Hodder and Stoughton, reprint 1944.

EADIE, JOHN. *A Commentary on the Greek Text of the Epistle of Paul to the Galatians*. Edinburgh: T & T Church, 1869.

FINDLAY, G. G. "Galatians," *The Expositor's Bible*, V. Grand Rapids: Wm. B. Eerdmans Publishing Co., 1956.

HOVEY, ALVAH. "Commentary on Galatians," *An American Commentary on the New Testament*, V. Philadelphia: American Baptist Publication Society, 1887.

LIGHTFOOT, J. B. *The Epistle of St. Paul to the Galatians*. Grand Rapids: Zondervan Publishing Co., reprint 1962.

MACLAREN, ALEXANDER. *Expositions of Holy Scripture*, XIV. Grand Rapids: Wm. B. Eerdmans Publishing Co., reprint 1944.

ROBERTSON, ARCHIBALD THOMAS. *Word Pictures in the New Testament*, IV. Nashville: Broadman Press, 1931.

WILLIAMS, A. LUKYN. *Galatians*. ("Cambridge Greek Testament.") Cambridge: The University Press, 1914.

WUEST, KENNETH S. *Galatians in Greek New Testament for the English Reader*. Grand Rapids: Wm. B. Eerdmans Publishing Co., 1944.